# THE MIND

# ‹THE MIND›

## 12 studies that unlocked the secrets of the unconscious

EDITED BY **Lucy Freeman**

THOMAS Y. CROWELL COMPANY

New York          Established 1834

Acknowledgment is made to the following sources: Josef Breuer and Sigmund Freud, *Studies on Hysteria* (Basic Books, Inc.); Robert P. Knight, "Intimidation of Others as a Defense Against Anxiety," in *Bulletin of the Menninger Clinic,* Vol. VI, No. 1 (January 1942); Ludwig Eidelberg, "A Bottle Broke," chapter in *Take Off Your Mask,* published in 1948 (Pyramid Books); Hyman Spotnitz, Leo Nagelberg, and Yonata Feldman for article in *The American Journal of Orthopsychiatry,* Vol. XXVI, No. 1 (January 1956); Melanie Klein, "An Obsessional Neurosis in a Six-Year-Old Girl," chapter in *The Psychoanalysis of Children,* Vol. XXII in International Psycho-Analytical Library (The Hogarth Press, Ltd.); Walter Stewart, abstract in *The Psychoanalytic Quarterly,* Vol. XXXX, No. 1 (January 1961); Dorothy Baruch, *One Little Boy* (Julian Press, Inc., Publishers); Martin Grotjahn, "Psychoanalytic Investigation of a Seventy-One-Year-Old Man with Senile Dementia," in *The Psychoanalytic Quarterly,* Vol. IX (1940); A. Sandor Lorand, "Crime and Fantasy," chapter in *Clinical Studies in Psychoanalysis,* published in 1950 (International Universities Press); Robert Lindner, *Rebel Without a Cause,* published in 1944 (Grune & Stratton, Inc.); Alexander Grainick, "The Carrington Family: A Psychiatric and Social Study Illustrating the Psychosis of Association or *Folie à Deux,* in *The Psychiatric Quarterly,* Vol. XVII (April 1943); Wulf Sachs, *Black Anger,* first published under this title in 1947 and later retitled *Black Hamlet* (Little, Brown and Co.).

*To Martin Mann*

# Preface

The birth of psychoanalysis generally is dated from the publication in 1895 of *Studies on Hysteria,* which contained five case studies —four by Sigmund Freud and the other by his friend and colleague, Josef Breuer. A year later, Freud coined the term "psychoanalysis" to describe the art-science he had founded.

Since Freud's initial discoveries in the treatment of emotional illness, the scope of psychoanalysis has widened. Freud began by treating a then relatively common illness, "hysteria"; today the psychoanalyst eases many ills of the troubled mind, ranging from mild anxieties to deep-seated delusions. His techniques are used to aid persons of all ages, from the very young child to the grandparent, and from all walks of life, from the teen-age delinquent to the Wall Street broker. When applied over a long period of time, modern psychoanalysis may even resolve conflicts that help cause alcoholism, criminal behavior, and homosexuality.

Freud himself elaborated, clarified, and in some instances changed his theories until his death in the fall of 1939. Like an artist, he first sketched the skeletal framework, then added to it— line by line, color by color—until he had constructed the complex, rich, many-faceted portrait of psychoanalysis. Sometimes it was difficult to find the right direction. He might deviate from a direction that seemed false or change its emphasis. However, as Dr. Walter A. Stewart points out in his book *Psychoanalysis: The First Ten Years,* to be published by The Macmillan Company in early 1968, Freud "never abandoned but rather modified the basic discoveries" of his early years.

Each of the cases in this book is tied closely to the underlying tenets of Freudian psychoanalysis. Some of the cases are well known, particularly those of Freud's, who in all wrote only ten long case histories. The cases by other psychoanalysts have appeared chiefly in technical books and journals. One was published as an abstract in a journal and is published here more fully for the first time. Some of the cases are not typical of the procedures of the classical psychoanalysts but, rather, represent psychotherapy based on psychoanalytic theory. Each case was selected because it seemed in some way to show another dimension of psychoanalysis.

Psychoanalytic treatment today is viewed more as a developmental process than, as Freud first believed, the uncovering of specific traumatic events in childhood, usually of a sexual nature. Psychoanalytic treatment is a process during which the patient grows emotionally. He becomes aware of the distorted fantasies of childhood that have caused his conflicts and he learns to cope with his emotions.

Even at the beginning, psychoanalysis was a complicated method of treatment, although the treatment usually lasted only a matter of months. The goals of psychoanalysis are now more ambitious and today psychoanalysis usually requires more time. The late Ernest Jones, who studied with Freud and wrote the three-volume biography *The Life and Work of Sigmund Freud,* once commented that the more we understand about the human mind, the longer psychoanalytic treatment will take.

Robert Waelder, a noted psychoanalyst, recently remarked, "There are no crash programs in psychoanalysis." Explaining that "it takes as much time for an embryo to develop in the space age as the ice age," he compared the process of psychoanalysis, as it is used by a person to explore his life and slowly change parts of it he does not like, to other life processes that cannot be hurried because they involve bodily and psychological growth.

Psychoanalysis is not static. As in other scientific fields, there will, no doubt, be changes and additions. But whatever discoveries lie ahead, they can only serve, as Dr. Leo Rangell, President of the American Psychoanalytic Association, has said, "to illuminate the human mind so man may have a greater say about his destiny."

*Lucy Freeman*

# Contents

# Chimney Sweeping

A colleague of Freud's, and a beautiful young woman whom Freud never saw, both helped lead the way to unveil secrets of the human mind. On November 18, 1882, thirteen years before the publication of *Studien über Hysterie* (*"Studies on Hysteria"*), Josef Breuer told Freud about a patient who had cured herself of severe physical and emotional illness by talking regularly to Breuer, during the period between 1880 and 1882, and confessing certain memories and emotions that shamed and upset her. She called this talking-out process "chimney sweeping." Her story was to profoundly influence Freud.

¶Freud left Vienna in 1885 to go to Paris, where he studied under the famed neurologist Charcot, who was in charge of the Salpêtrière, an ancient fortress of an asylum for the mentally ill. Upon returning to Vienna the following year, Freud began to specialize in cases of nervous diseases, the most common of which was hysteria. Hysteria now is classified as a psychoneurosis, an emotional disturbance in which, for no apparent organic reason, the patient suffers from compulsions, obsessions, or phobias in combination with such physical symptoms as fainting, headaches, or paralysis. Early analytic techniques were believed applicable to this type of illness, but not to the more serious psychoses in which an individual's personality was so disorganized that the person was completely incapable of leading a normal life.

At the time Freud began treating hysteria, the general practice among doctors in such cases was to advise medication, massage, a change of scenery, or slight electric shock. Some doctors, Freud included, used hypnosis. While the patient was hypnotized they would make such suggestions as, "you will feel less nervous on waking" or "you will no longer have headaches when you wake up." Sometimes this worked but only temporarily; usually the patient was back in the doctor's office suffering from the same symptoms.

Not satisfied with these temporary results, Freud started to use hypnosis for another purpose. He had noticed that patients while hypnotized were able to recall thoughts unavailable to them while awake. So, instead of making suggestions while under hypnosis, he asked his patients to talk about their memories, using hypnosis to produce what he called "catharsis." Freud hoped that through catharsis patients could relate their memories to their emotional conflicts and thus solve their problems.

Freud believed that certain experiences, although forgotten and relegated to the unconscious—which he called the storehouse of memory—were the cause of the symptoms of hysteria—the migraine headaches, paralysis of arms and legs, facial twitching, and other such symptoms for which no physical cause could be found. At first, astonished that patients could easily recall dates, names, and numbers supposedly forgotten for years, Freud thought this was proof of the accuracy and power of memory.

Freud thought that patients really knew everything that related psychologically to their physical illness and would eventually communicate it to the doctor if they mentioned every single thought that entered their minds and thus unveiled their buried memories. He was also very interested in finding out why their memory had been hidden from consciousness.

At first Freud asked patients while hypnotized to tell him all they could about memories that related to the particular physical symptom from which they suffered. Then he became dissatisfied with hypnosis. In *An Autobiographical Study* he explained that he gave up hypnosis because it "had screened from view an interplay of forces which now came into sight and the understanding of which gave a solid foundation" to his theory that buried memories were the cause of the illness.

He called this new method "concentration"—concentration without hypnosis on the symptom. When that, too, did not satisfy him, as though remembering Anna O.'s "chimney sweeping," talking about whatever she wished day after day, he asked patients to "free associate," as he called it, as they lay on the couch. (He believed that lying down relaxed a person so he could talk more freely.)

Between the years 1892 and 1895, Freud developed the technique of free association. He found that as patients were able to speak of every thought that occurred, no matter how frightening, embarrassing, or shameful they believed it to be, they uncovered and faced the wishes and fears that had caused their emotional and physical distress.

Freud felt he was on the right track. This was a hard-won victory for him, for doctors were not supposed to listen to patients—they were supposed to do the talking and tell the patient what to do. Freud had to overcome his own medical training, as well as any tendency in himself to be the dictator, and be willing to listen.

He proved not only willing but eager to hear what his patients had to say, and with his great perception and understanding of human emotions, he discovered what no man before had been able to do—how to heal the human mind by uncovering the unconscious fears and wishes of the mind.

It was not only what a patient said, but the tone of his voice and even his slightest movement on the couch as he talked—or remained silent—that Freud used in exploring the unconscious. He once said, "Betrayal oozes from every pore," meaning that the patient betrayed unconscious feelings with his every gesture.

Realizing the value of free association, Freud persuaded Breuer to collaborate with him in describing the case of Anna O. for the medical world (her real name was later revealed as Bertha Pappenheim, a wealthy woman who spent the rest of her life in philanthropic work in Germany). The case first appeared in a joint paper published in 1893 entitled "The Psychical Mechanism of Hysterical Phenomena," and later, in 1895, it became part of the book *Studies on Hysteria*.

Freud's four cases were Frau Emmy, whom he treated in 1889 by hypnosis, Fraulein Elisabeth von R. and Miss Lucy R., treated in 1892 by the "concentration" method, and Katharina, an eighteen-year-old girl who asked for help one day when he was vacationing in the Alps.

In these four cases and six others that he subsequently published Freud displayed his remarkable literary talent. (He received the Goethe Prize for Literature—a high honor—at Frankfurt in 1930.) His description of theory is clear and eloquent, and humor is often used as part of his explanation. His writing style as shown in his ten clinical cases, a few of which run almost two hundred pages and read like novels, has not been excelled in the field of psychoanalysis to this day.

In the case of Miss Lucy R., Freud dramatically illustrated the nature of "repression," which he described as the "foundation-stone on which the whole structure of psychoanalysis rests." Miss Lucy R. was a young English governess who sought Freud's help, a courageous thing for her to do in moralistic Victorian Vienna, just as it was courageous for Freud to express his revolutionary views. Although most doctors at that time scoffed at Freud's belief that the mind had anything to do with illnesses of the body there was one who, having failed to help the governess, suggested she consult Freud. (Freud was then in his sixth year of practice in Vienna.)

Miss Lucy R. complained that the membranes inside her nose were swollen and she had trouble breathing, symptoms of a nasal condition known as rhinitis. She also suffered from an occasional hallucination that she smelled certain strong odors even though she had lost her sense of smell. (Undoubtedly the physical swelling of the membranes of the nose did contribute to this hysterical symptom.) She also had severe headaches and loss of appetite, and became easily tired, often sinking into a state of depression. This made it difficult for her to take care of her two charges, the small daughters of a widower, a hard-driving businessman who was the director of a factory in outer Vienna.

After interviewing her, Freud diagnosed her condition as a case of mild hysteria. In her first session, she spoke of being tormented by the sensations of strong odors that occurred without warning every so often. Freud decided to make this the starting point of the analysis. He asked what odor she smelled most often, and she replied, burnt pudding.

During the sessions that followed, Freud uncovered the fact that she had first smelled burnt pudding two months before, two days prior to her birthday. She had been cooking for her two small charges when she received a letter from her mother in Glasgow. She wanted to read it then, but the children tore it out of her hands and insisted that she wait to read it on her birthday. While they were teasing her she suddenly became aware of a strong odor: the pudding she was cooking had been forgotten and was burning. Ever since she had been pursued by the smell; it became stronger when she felt upset.

Although fond of the children, she told Freud she had given notice to her employer. He had advised her, in a friendly way, to think it over for a few weeks, and because of her uncertainty, she had stayed on. She also felt disturbed because if she left she would be breaking a deathbed promise made to the children's mother (a distant relative of hers) that she would devote herself to the children and take their mother's place.

Freud thus connected the smell of burnt pudding to an actual experience in her life, an experience associated with what he called "a little scene" in which opposing conflicts—to leave or not to leave the children—were reawakened when she received the letter from her mother. The sensation of smell associated with these conflicts persisted, symbolic of the "scene," even though she had buried all emotions connected with it because they were painful.

But it was still necessary, he believed, to explain why, out of all the emotions evoked by the experience, Miss Lucy R. had chosen the smell of burnt pudding to symbolize it. He asked how she had been feeling at that time, and she said that she had been suffering from such a bad cold that she was unable to smell anything. Yet the smell of burnt pudding reached her nose and Freud wondered why; he was not satisfied with her explanation.

He wanted to know why her conflicts had led to her particular symptoms—loss of the sense of smell and fatigue; why she suffered bodily pain because of a psychological trauma; and why the smell of burnt pudding came back to her but not the memory of the scene itself.

Freud already knew from analyzing similar cases that, in hysteria, one essential condition had to be fulfilled: an idea had to be *intentionally repressed from consciousness*. This intentional repression was the basis for the conversion of the psychic energy into a physical symptom as the energy cut off from the psychic association found an outlet, stimulating some part of the body.

Freud believed the basis for Miss Lucy R.'s repression could only stem from some deep feeling of displeasure or discomfort—a basic incompatibility between the idea that had to be repressed and the maintenance of her self-respect. But the repressed idea, instead of staying buried, took revenge in various ways, causing her physical symptoms.

What lay behind the memory of the burnt pudding? What did Miss Lucy R. *not* want to recall and had intentionally repressed? She seemed truly fond of the children. She was also very sensitive to the opinion of other members of the household as to her character—she revealed that she was leaving because she thought they were talking against her to her employer and his father and that she was not getting as much support from the two men as she had expected.

Only one conclusion could be reached, Freud said, and he was "bold enough" to mention it. He told Miss Lucy R. that he believed she was in love with her employer, although she was perhaps unaware of her feelings, and that she nourished a secret wish to take his dead wife's place. She was also afraid the servants had guessed this and were making fun of her.

Miss Lucy R. admitted, in what Freud called "her usual laconic fashion," "Yes, I think that's true."

Freud asked in astonishment why, if she knew she loved her employer, she had not mentioned it before.

She replied, "I didn't know—or rather I didn't want to know. I wanted to drive it out of my head and not think of it again; and I believe latterly I have succeeded." Freud commented later that he had "never managed to give a better description than this of the strange state in which one knows and does not know a thing at the same time."

He then asked her why she was unwilling to admit her feelings, whether she was ashamed of loving a man. She answered that it was distressing to her because the man was her employer, and because she was a poor girl and he a rich man from a good family. She thought people would laugh at her if they knew of her ideas.

She went on to tell Freud that for the first few years she had lived happily in the house, but one day her employer, whose behavior toward her had always been very reserved, started to discuss the children with her and seemed far more friendly than usual. He told her how much he depended on her for the care of his motherless daughters. As he said this, she thought "he looked at her meaningly." At that moment she allowed herself to feel her hidden love. She dared hope they would grow closer, but he had never attempted to talk to her on a personal level again and she had made up her mind to banish all thoughts of love between them. She admitted to Freud that there was little likelihood he thought of her as a second wife.

Freud expected that, with this new awareness, Miss Lucy R. would feel better, but she continued to complain about being depressed. The imaginary smell of burnt pudding did not disappear completely, although it grew weaker and occurred only when she felt anxious.

The persistence of the smell led Freud to believe that it was associated with other, deeper conflicts she had repressed. He kept asking her to talk about anything that might have to do with burnt pudding. She mentioned the children's grandfather and family quarrels that had occurred in her presence.

About this time her nasal disorder became so severe that she canceled treatment temporarily. It was the Christmas season and, on her return, she told Freud she had received a great many presents from her employer and his father, and even from the servants, as though they all wanted to make up to her for the unpleasantness of the past few months. But she had not been impressed with the gifts, she said.

Freud asked again about the smell of burnt pudding. She said it had disappeared, but that now she was troubled by another smell—cigar smoke. She recalled that it, too, had been present earlier but had been overwhelmed by the stronger smell of burnt pudding.

Here Freud noted, in his description of the case, that one symptom might be removed only to have its place taken by another, and that symptom after symptom had to be pursued until the underlying cause became known. So he began work on the second symptom, hoping to uncover its cause. He asked if there were any occasions Miss Lucy R. remembered smelling cigar smoke.

Speaking hesitantly, she recalled a scene in the dining room. There had been a guest, the chief accountant at her employer's factory, an old man who was very fond of the children and who often came to lunch. As the children said good-bye after eating, the accountant tried to kiss them, but their father became furious and shouted at him not to kiss them. Miss Lucy R. felt, she said, a stab at her heart. At that moment the men were smoking, she recalled, and the cigar smoke stuck in her memory.

Thus she had remembered a second, deeper-lying experience, which, like the first, was painful to her and had been banished from her mind. But *why* was it so painful, Freud wondered? He asked her which of the two scenes had occurred first, the one associated with the burnt pudding or the cigar smoke? She said the one associated with the cigar smoke had happened two months earlier.

Freud then asked why, when her employer reprimanded the old man, she felt the stab in her heart, since she herself was not involved. She replied that she didn't feel it was right for him to shout at an old man, who was a good friend of his and a guest in his house.

She remarked that her employer had never liked anyone to kiss his children, and then the memory of a third and even earlier experience emerged. A few months before this, she recalled, a woman friend of her employer's came to visit and, as she was leaving, kissed the children on the lips. The father saw her do this and said nothing to the woman, but, after she left, he turned his fury on Miss Lucy R. He said he would hold her responsible if anyone kissed his children on the lips, that it was her duty not to allow it, and if it ever happened again he would fire her and get someone else to take care of them.

She was shocked. This had happened when she still thought it possible he might care for her, and his words doomed all her hopes. She told herself she must have made a mistake, for he could never have had any deep feeling toward her or he would have treated her with more consideration.

This was the true trauma and it was because of it, Freud noted, that the experience with the chief accountant had seemed so devastating.

Two days after this session, Miss Lucy R. visited Freud again, and she was smiling and happy. Thinking that perhaps her employer had proposed marriage, he asked what had happened.

She said nothing had happened. It was just that Freud did not know her as she really was—that she was cheerful as a rule. When Freud asked how she felt about her prospects in the house, she replied that she knew she had none and didn't intend to make herself miserable over it, and that she had given up all ideas of her employer loving her.

Upon examining her nose, Freud found its state to be almost normal; she was now able to distinguish between smells if they were strong.

Her treatment ran for a total of nine weeks. Freud reported that four months later he met her by chance in a summer resort and she seemed in good spirits, assuring him that her nose did not trouble her any more.

Miss Lucy R. had tried to forget the painful memory of having the man she wished would love her expressing anger toward her, and had also tried to bury all thoughts of her love for him since she could not bear to recognize the fact that her love was hopeless. In doing so, she had developed a physical illness, had been subject to hallucinations about smells, and had become depressed.

Through this case Freud was able to give clear and simple evidence of the purpose of repression, as well as how repressed emotions return in different forms. Miss Lucy R. had tried to hide the memory of an experience which, in its recollection, brought only pain and embarrassment. Her psychic distress was transformed into physical symptoms, a process Freud called "conversion," wherein body and mind interacted in the interests of emotional survival.

Another one of Freud's theories, the most controversial of all at the start of his career, was his belief that neurosis in adults could be caused by repressed memories of sexual assaults suffered as children.

He illustrated this theory in *Studies on Hysteria* with the case of Katharina, who had repressed the memory of an early attempted sexual assault. (He explained that he did not consider this brief exploration of a young woman's fears and memories to be a "psychoanalysis" in any sense of the word. He said he had tried "a lucky guess" as to the psychic cause of her physical illness.)

Freud met Katharina while he was vacationing in the Alps. He had left the lodge where he was staying to climb one of the mountains and at the top, had sat down to rest and enjoy the view.

Suddenly he heard a voice ask if he were a doctor. He turned to see "the rather sulky-looking girl" of about eighteen who served his meals at the lodge. She had followed him up the mountain.

The landlady had addressed her as "Katharina," and he judged by her dress and manner that she could not be a servant but was somehow related to the owner of the lodge. (In the original version of the case, Freud described the landlady and her husband as Katharina's "aunt" and "uncle." A number of years later, when he felt there was no longer any need to protect the girl's anonymity, he revealed that the "aunt" and "uncle" were actually her mother and father.)

After Freud admitted that he was a doctor, she asked if he had a few moments to spare, saying she needed his help because her nerves were bad. One doctor she had consulted had given her some medicine, but it had proved useless.

Freud asked what she was suffering from. When she said she got so out of breath that sometimes she felt she would suffocate, he realized she was describing what he called an anxiety attack. He had discovered that in such instances a person often would choose one of the many physical sensations prompted by anxiety and focus on it. He asked Katharina to tell him about any other physical sensations she experienced when she felt out of breath. She mentioned a pressing on her eyes, a heaviness in her head, a buzzing sound in her ears, and a fear that someone would catch hold of her. At these moments, she said, she thought she was "going to die."

Freud asked if she thought of anything or saw anything when she had the attacks. She replied that she always saw a frightening face that looked at her angrily. When Freud asked if she recognized the face, she said she did not. Then he asked when she had first suffered such an attack; she said about two years earlier, and that they had been recurring ever since.

It was then that Freud tried what he later called a "lucky guess," based on his findings that girls often experienced anxiety when they faced the world of sensuality for the first time. He told

Katharina she must have seen or heard something that embarrassed her very much and which she would rather not have known about.

At this suggestion Katharina promptly remembered the time she had "caught" her uncle with her cousin, Franziska. It was a day when her aunt, then operating a lodge in another part of the valley, had gone out and a customer asked for something to eat. Katharina looked all over for Franziska, who did the cooking, but could not find her. She then searched for her uncle, but he, too, was absent. When her little cousin Alois suggested that Franziska might be in their uncle's room, they went there and found the door locked, which seemed strange to her.

Alois then suggested they look into the room from a window in the passageway, but after they entered the passage, he would not go to the window, saying he was afraid. Katharina, however, had not been afraid, and had looked in. The room was dark but she could see her uncle lying on top of Franziska in the bed.

Afterward, she walked away from the window and leaned against a wall, unable to get her breath. She said, "Everything went blank, my eyelids were forced together and there was a . . . buzzing in my head." She had felt very frightened.

Freud asked why she had been so frightened—had she understood what she saw? She said she had not, that she was then only sixteen and did not know why she had been frightened, and that she had forgotten all her thoughts while she was experiencing the attack. When Freud asked if the face she always saw when she lost her breath was Franziska's, she replied it was the face of a man. Freud then asked if it could be her uncle's. She answered that it had been too dark in the room for her to see his face. (Apparently she was trying to deny to herself that it was her uncle who was involved.)

Her memory now seemed blocked, but Freud hoped she might reveal more if she kept talking. He asked what happened next. She said that her uncle and cousin must have heard something because they came out of the room shortly. All that day she felt sick when she thought about what she had seen. Three days later she started to feel even sicker and stayed in bed for three days, vomiting constantly.

Freud thought of his research with anxiety attacks and recalled that when a woman vomited it usually meant she felt disgust. He told Katharina that he believed her three-day sickness indicated that she had felt disgusted when she looked into the room. Katharina agreed, but said she did not know why she felt that way. Freud suggested that perhaps it was because she had seen someone naked. She repeated that it had been too dark to see anything, but then added that both Franziska and her uncle had been clothed.

She told him that her aunt had sensed she was hiding a secret and that she had finally revealed to her aunt what she had seen. After that there were angry scenes between her uncle and aunt, and finally her aunt left with her children and niece, and took over the lodge where Freud was staying. Franziska, who had become pregnant, stayed with Katharina's uncle.

In the middle of Katharina's account of the separation and subsequent divorce of her aunt and uncle, for which she blamed herself, she drifted back to earlier memories, much to Freud's astonishment. She recalled that two or three years before the traumatic scene between her cousin and uncle, her uncle had made sexual advances to her.

When Katharina was fourteen, she had spent a winter's night with her uncle at an inn in the valley. He had stayed in the bar, drinking and playing cards, while she went upstairs to bed in the room they were to share. She had just fallen asleep when she woke suddenly, feeling his body in the bed. She jumped up and asked him what he was up to, why he did not stay in his own bed. He tried to calm her, calling her a silly girl, and telling her she didn't know how nice sex was. She told him she didn't like his "nice" things and that he didn't let anyone sleep in peace. She stood by the door, ready to dash into the hall should he make further advances, but finally he went over to his own bed and fell asleep.

Freud asked Katharina if she had known what her uncle was

trying to do. She denied that she had known at the time, although it had become clear to her much later. "She had resisted because it was unpleasant to be disturbed in one's sleep and 'because it wasn't 'nice.' "

She then spoke of further sexual experiences with her uncle. In an inn on another evening, she had had to defend herself against him when he was very drunk. Still another night, when they were staying at an inn where she and her uncle were sleeping in one room and Franziska in an adjoining one, she had awakened to see her uncle turning the handle of the door. When she asked what he was doing, he said he was looking for something.

When Freud asked Katharina if she had been frightened during those episodes, she replied that she thought so but was not sure.

When she was able to recall the unpleasant memories, Freud noted: "She was like someone transformed." Her sullen, unhappy face took on a bright, lively look. Freud believed that her case had become clear to him. What she had told him, in apparently aimless fashion, had provided an "admirable explanation," he said, for her behavior when she had discovered her uncle and cousin in sexual intercourse: she had established an immediate connection between the sight and what had happened previously in her own life. Her vomiting had been caused not by disgust at the sight of the two in bed, but by the memory it stirred up within her.

This case furthered Freud's belief in the "seduction" theory as the cause of neurosis, an erroneous concept which he corrected a few years later. The "seduction" theory was, however, a momentous discovery, for it had only to be reversed—the wish for seduction on the part of the child, not an actual seduction—to lead to his important theory of infantile sexuality.

Many of his women patients told Freud that they had been seduced by their fathers and at first he believed all of them. Gradually, however, he realized that many women only imagined such seductions, which led him to the theory that the seductions represented the natural wish of every child to possess the parent of the opposite sex and do away with the parent of the same sex. He called this the Oedipus complex, after the hero of the Greek tragedy who unknowingly killed his father and married his mother.

He also concluded that a sexually stimulating experience could affect future psychic development, even if the child were too young to understand fully what had occurred. The experience could always unconsciously haunt the person and release disturbing feelings. Thus, there could be a delayed reaction to a traumatic event of earlier years.

Among the six long case histories that Freud published after *Studies on Hysteria* was one called "Analysis of a Phobia in a Five-Year-Old Boy," which bore out Freud's theory that sexuality did not spring full-blown in the adult but had its roots in childhood. Freud's report on little Hans, the first psychoanalytic study of a child, was published in 1909. In this case, Freud himself saw the patient only once during the analysis, which actually was carried out by the child's father. The general lines of the treatment, however, were laid down by Freud, and the father conferred frequently with him about the child's progress.

Freud maintained that children, far from being the little innocents that everyone thought, were extremely conscious of their sexual feelings. He used the word "sexual" in this instance, he said, to mean awareness of the functions and appearance of their bodies and curiosity about the bodies of their parents, about how babies are conceived and born, and about the act of sex. If they slept in their parents' bedroom and happened to see or hear their parents in sexual intercourse, they might then become overstimulated and need to defend themselves against this excess stimulation.

These ideas, which Freud published in *Three Essays on the Theory of Sexuality* in 1905, brought down on him the skepticism and wrath of the world—including most of the medical profession.

Freud also produced startling insights into the depths of man's nature in each of his five other lengthy clinical cases. In the case of the Rat Man, known as such because it involved a young man's fantasy about rats and entitled "Notes on a Case of Obsessional Neurosis" (1909), are shown causes of obsessional behavior. Freud pointed out that those suffering from obsessions were terrified that their wishes would come true, as though the wish were the same as the deed.

In the case of Dora, which Freud entitled "Fragment of an Analysis of a Case of Hysteria" (1905), he illustrated the value of interpreting dreams in analytic treatment (he called dreams "the royal road to the unconscious"). The case entitled "Psycho-Analytic Notes on an Autobiographical Account of a Case of Paranoia" (1911), or the Schreber case, set forth Freud's theory that paranoia is a defense against homosexuality.

In "The Psychogenesis of a Case of Female Homosexuality" (1914), Freud concluded that the woman homosexual does not work out her rivalry with her mother for the love of her father, a love which she then would normally transfer to another man. Instead, she acts the way many people do when they are disappointed in love, and identify with the lost object, thereby, according to Freud, finding a way of avoiding conflict with the mother. The young woman he was writing about had attempted suicide at one point; Freud presented his theory that suicide is also unconscious murder since no one can find the psychical energy to kill himself unless he is unconsciously killing someone with whom he is identifying.

"From the History of an Infantile Neurosis" (1918) contained the study of a childhood neurosis resurrected through the psycho-analysis of an adult neurosis, and showed that childhood memories could be recaptured through analysis in later life. Freud theorized from it that every adult neurosis is built on a childhood one.

In these cases Freud illustrated most of his famous theories. The theories were borne out in cases written up by psychoanalysts who followed Freud.

# The "Fearless" Coward

The need to love and be loved is universal. Both men and women have feelings of love (and hate) not only for members of the opposite sex but the same sex. These feelings enable us to form friendships, to work together in harmony, and to socialize with our own sex.

But some deny these feelings because they are frightened of them. They see them only at the sexual level. The need to love or be loved by a member of the same sex means to them "homosexuality," an evil from which they must flee.

In the treatment of the homosexual, or those so disturbed by their feelings about the same sex that they cannot function well in life, psychoanalysts have found that violence may serve to cover up awareness of the desire for a homosexual attachment. Unprovoked hostility and a slight sense of paranoia (they go together), as Freud said, may be a defense against homosexuality.

This is shown in the following case, originally entitled "Intimidation of Others as a Defense Against Anxiety," written by the late Dr. Robert P. Knight who was medical director of Austen Riggs Center, Stockbridge, Massachusetts. [It originally appeared in the *Bulletin of the Menninger Clinic,* Vol. VI, No. 1 (January 1942).] The "sanatorium" referred to is the Menninger Clinic.

¶The patient was a young man, a twenty-year-old college engineering student, who had a nervous breakdown while undergoing the hazing of "hell week" as a fraternity pledge.

Dr. Knight saw him at the sanatorium for a total of 250 analytic hours during fourteen months. The patient's father, a pharmacist, was irascible and hypochondriacal and his mother was an unstable woman. They fought almost continually and the patient, as a child, frequently was drawn into their battles. The patient had a brother, three years younger. From early childhood, the patient had collected guns, gone shooting a great deal, and had been active in football and boxing. In college, he took military training.

For several years he had difficulty waking up in the morning. If someone shook him, as frequently happened in the fraternity house, he would jump out of bed and stand on guard with fists clenched, ready to defend himself against attack. A shower would thoroughly wake him, otherwise he might go for several hours before suddenly "coming to" and realizing what he was doing, although he appeared to act normally. One morning he ate breakfast, attended four classes, had lunch, and began to play tennis before he suddenly "came to" and was aware that he did not remember a thing he had done. Every night before going to sleep, he drank large amounts of water, believing he was washing out his system. This meant he had to get up and urinate many times during the night. Also, he always went to sleep with an erection. This had started at the age of ten, at which time he had been circumcised, a traumatic experience for any boy that age. When feeling unsure of himself and self-conscious in a crowd, he always got an erection and then felt more secure.

During "hell week," he resented becoming a servant to upperclassmen. One evening after he had been routed out of bed to run an errand, he returned to his room and sat up all night at his drawing board, unaware of his surroundings. A few days later, he fell over backward in his chair and lay unconscious for several hours. When he revived, he struck out viciously at some of the fraternity members and seemed not to recognize them or his family who were hastily summoned, and whom he also tried to attack. He was put into a general hospital because doctors thought he had injured his head in the fall. But the neurological examination proved negative.

He continued to shadow box with unseen enemies, to operate an imaginary machine gun, and to prepare for battle at the approach of any doctor who tried to examine him. After a brief stay at home he was brought to the sanatorium by his father. On entering he announced threateningly that he was not going to stand for any nonsense.

When Dr. Knight started the analysis he noticed the young man carried one shoulder a little higher than the other and that he frequently raised one eyebrow and lowered the other in what he apparently regarded as an intimidating expression.

During the first hour of analysis the young man insisted on sitting up, declared he did not intend to take anything from anybody, and that he had hundreds of fights and each time his opponent came off second best. At the same time he told the analyst he wanted help with his problems.

At the second session, he deigned to half-recline on the couch as he talked. Dr. Knight asked about his reactions to the first session, particularly his reactions to the analyst, since Dr. Knight noted that the young man had been watching closely every move the analyst made. The young man replied that he had noticed the analyst's size (Dr. Knight was a very tall, well-built man) and thought he seemed rather heavy and athletically inclined. Dr. Knight asked how he felt when meeting a new man. He replied that he always sized the new man up immediately in regard to the possible outcome of a fight.

The young man became irritated when Dr. Knight started to ask questions about his past. He said sharply that the information was all on the record and could be found there. Dr. Knight told him that he was always to express anger when he felt it. The young man laughed and said that no one need worry about that.

Dr. Knight remarked that the young man seemed highly conscious of weapons of attack and defense, alert to any possible encroachment on his rights, and ready to do battle if unfairly treated. Dr. Knight commended him on his attitude of determination and self-assertion but pointed out that, at the same time, these characteristics seemed to be overdeveloped to the point of overwhelming him with excitement or unconsciousness at times. Dr. Knight suggested that it might be that the young man was driven to the need to be belligerent because of some past experiences and influences, and that it was important to discover everything possible about them. The young man seemed to accept this.

The patient began the third session by saying that he had been thinking about how he felt on meeting men, because of Dr. Knight's comments of the day before, and he was surprised by his strong emotions. He said that almost every night he dreamed of fights in which he annihilated other men. Ever since he was seven, he had fantasies about how he would meet attacks—where he would hide, from behind what barricades he would fire his revolvers and machine guns, where he would build forts for emergency protection, and from what direction the enemy most likely would appear. He never traveled to the city or country, nor did he ever enter a strange building, without considering where possible enemies might lurk and what maneuvers he would make if attacked. After he began to study military science, the tactical details of these fantasies became even more elaborate.

The next weekend the young man left the sanatorium without permission and went to a nearby city to visit a cousin with whom he discussed at length his parents' constant quarreling. He telephoned the sanatorium to notify officials that he would return Sunday evening, and was good to his word. At his appointment with Dr. Knight on Monday morning, he announced threateningly that he was not going to put up with any nonsense about discipline, and that he would stand for no punishment because he had broken a rule. Dr. Knight told him that he knew of no intended action but that, if it were decided by the hospital doctors that any was indicated for his best interests, action would be taken.

The young man replied that he knew he could not intimidate the entire staff. If anything were done to him, somebody would get hurt, he warned, and sooner or later he would escape and neither the doctors nor his family would ever hear of him again. Dr. Knight remarked that the young man seemed to be acting like Don Quixote attacking windmills, since no one had said a word about disciplining him. Actually, no restrictions were imposed. The doctors felt that if punishment were imposed, the patient might be forced to carry out his threats in order to save face, thus breaking the rapport Dr. Knight had established with him and delaying the course of treatment.

Dr. Knight noticed that his patient's shadow boxing and pretended machine gunning of people had disappeared, and that he now seemed to act fairly normal. But his loud, blustering voice, his demands to have his wishes granted, and his threats to annihilate anyone who infringed upon his rights, continued.

During the following analytic sessions, the young man described more of his past aggressive activities. He had been carrying and shooting revolvers and rifles since the age of ten. He told of a new invention on which he was working to improve machine guns so that bullets would feed into the gun at four times the standard rate, thus enormously increasing the kill power. His tone was serious when he discussed this, but Dr. Knight noted that he smiled when he remarked that he had long ago taken care of the fortifications around the sanatorium. Dr. Knight was pleased by the young man's smile for it meant he was developing some humor about his aggressiveness, aware of its extreme extent.

The young man now began to talk about his feelings of insecurity. He said he once was religious and still prayed every night, but was afraid he had lost his feeling for religion. For some months he had been trying to convince himself that he had no need of religion, or affection from anyone. However, now he felt he might be mistaken, he said. He was also afraid he might go "stir crazy" and that he might just "babble" during the analytic hour.

One of the girl patients seemed interested in him but her affection was not enough, he said. When he had discovered he could not get much affection at home, he had expected some at college and was very upset when he had to suffer the indignities that accompanied being a fraternity pledge. Dr. Knight learned that his first attack of stupor had occurred after he had resentfully obeyed the order of an upperclassman. The second took place after he had complained about a low grade to what he called "a prissy English professor." He thought the professor was a homosexual, felt very antagonistic toward him, and had become very angry with him.

Since the young man spoke at some length and with deep scorn about the professor as a homosexual, Dr. Knight asked him casually what he thought about homosexuals. The young man then told of several incidents where men had attempted to seduce him. In each case, he said, he had knocked the man down. Dr. Knight then asked if he thought his readiness to attack men might be related to his feelings about homosexuality. The young man did not answer.

The following session, however, he told Dr. Knight that he thought this observation was correct. He said he always felt tense when another boy put his hands on him or got chummy in any way. He said as a boy he had been taught to masturbate by a homosexual but had stopped masturbating years ago. He regarded masturbation as a homosexual activity.

The following hour the young man was very tense. He lit a cigarette, half-reclined on the couch, and remained silent. Dr. Knight asked him to talk about his feelings concerning the previous session. The young man said that now he could see no connection between homosexuality and his readiness to fight other men.

Dr. Knight explained that when an idea occurs that is unwelcome, unpleasant, or intolerable, one way to fight it is to over-react against it. Whereupon the young man turned on his side, half-arose from the couch, glared at Dr. Knight and said that if the analyst was making any insinuations about him, he would punch him in the nose. Dr. Knight replied that such a reaction was confirmation they were dealing with something important. He said that he was not alarmed by the threat, having no interest in making accusations or insinuations but simply in discovering what was troubling the young man.

He asked the young man not to lose his perspective so easily in regard to the purposes of analysis or they would not find out much about the causes of his illness.

The young man then turned on his stomach and stretched out, looking up at Dr. Knight. He said he was interested in going on with the analysis. He spoke of being depressed, then of playing a game of tennis in which he was hit accidentally with a ball as his partner was serving. The partner (another patient of Dr. Knight's) apologized, but a little later, when the former partner became his opponent, he smashed a lob directly at him, hitting him in the abdomen and doubling him up. The young man did not apologize. He felt pleased at his retaliation. He said he had no scruples while playing football about stepping on the faces of other players. This had been done to him and everyone had to look out for himself.

Dr. Knight pointed out the possible connection between the young man's feelings of depression and his somewhat ruthless aggression against people who had not intentionally harmed him. The young man was silent. He left the hour early, saying he was not sure he could go on with the analysis. Dr. Knight said he hoped that the young man would continue and explained that there were bound to be difficult periods. However, he added, the young man would have to decide for himself, since it was his wish to get well that provided the motivation for continuance of the analysis.

During the next session, the young man told how after the previous hour he had returned to his room, cursed, kicked the wastebasket viciously, struck the walls with his fist, but finally decided that if he was supposed to have courage enough to fight and play football, he ought to have courage enough for analysis. He then confessed he had lied about masturbation. He had not quit as he had told Dr. Knight. He got so tense sometimes that he either had to fight somebody or masturbate, since either act would relieve the tension.

He recalled that when he was fourteen he once fought with his father. His parents had been quarreling violently and he protested. His father struck him, knocking him down. He got up from the floor and told his father that if he ever touched him or his mother again he would "blow him to hell." He loaded his .45 revolver, kept it loaded and ready for two years, and his father knew it and never touched him again, he said.

In college, during target practice, he often visualized the commanding officer as the target, and also felt sorry the targets were not living men. He thought that if he flunked out of college, he could become a criminal, a "trigger man." It might be hard the first time he killed a man but after that it would be easy, he said.

He complained that his analytic hours were not providing him with much relief but instead his tension seemed to be increasing. Dr. Knight told him that the more he could speak of his feelings, the more relief he would eventually get, and that perhaps he would not feel at ease until he understood the reason for his combativeness and hostility.

In a succeeding session, the young man related a dream of two years before which, he said, was the most frightening experience he ever had. He was then living at home and dreamed he was in bed, sleeping face down. A "terrifying-looking person" came into the room, all lighted up with candles like a Christmas tree. The intruder had "a terrible expression" on his face. He walked over to the young man and stabbed him three times in the back. The young man could feel the pain. He awoke, jumped out of bed, got his gun from the bureau drawer and stood trembling in the middle of the room trying to decide whether or not to shoot. He finally realized there was no one in the room and that it had been a dream.

In talking about his associative thoughts to the dream, he recalled spending one Christmas with a friend of the family who had been his camp counselor. He had slept in the same bed with this man when the latter visited his home and the man had made sexual advances, whereupon he jumped out of bed and struck the man in the face. He said he would fight anyone who implied he was a "pansy" or sissy, or in any way weak or effeminate.

Dr. Knight commented that every person has some traits which are weak, effeminate, or childish. The young man would not accept such an idea as applied to him. Instead, he became very angry at Dr. Knight and again spoke of fighting him.

The next session he described a dream of the night before. In it, he had come upon one of the doctors making love to a nurse. The doctor had an enormous penis. The young man was furious and knocked the doctor down.

In his associations to the dream, he confessed that he felt his own penis was quite small and that he had always been concerned about its size. He wondered if his ambition to be a fighter might be overcompensation for what he thought a lack of masculinity in himself.

He told of having been hypnotized five times three years before. He said it was after this that he had experienced difficulty waking up in the morning. Dr. Knight asked about this paradox between the young man's submission to a male hypnotist and his resentment against masculine authority. The young man replied that the hypnotism had merely been an experiment. But he seemed, according to Dr. Knight, to have gained some insight into the passive wishes involved in submitting to hypnotism.

Dr. Knight pointed out to him his conflict between his need for affection from a man, which he seemed to consider a weakness, and his fear of infringement of his rights by the man's authority. Dr. Knight said the young man displayed this attitude in the analysis, that while he regarded the analyst as a helping friend, still he watched him out of the corner of his eye while lying on the couch and was always ready to jump up. If the analyst made a slight noise while shifting position in his chair, the young man became alert and tense.

In discussing the case, Dr. Knight commented that it was obvious to him that, at this time, the young man was struggling with conscious, passive homosexual wishes and beset with fears about them. He was also holding back some disturbing experiences, undoubtedly of a homosexual character, Dr. Knight said. Throughout the sessions, as an analyst he had been consistently friendly, somewhat paternal, and had spoken always in a mild voice, expressing interpretations as tentative questions as he tried to draw out the fears which caused the young man's combative defenses and intimidating attitude. At this time the young man seemed to be getting more tense. He complained about not having enough active outlets. He asked the sanatorium staff to provide him with a sparring partner. He demanded sedatives to relieve his tension.

After he had boxed with an attendant and another patient, at the next session he abruptly asked Dr. Knight what sexual implications there were in boxing and wrestling. Dr. Knight explained the relationship, as he said, "cautiously," stating that sexual feelings might be part of the aggressiveness of punching and wrestling. The young man replied that this did not apply to him. Then he told of another incident when a homosexual had tried to seduce him and he had knocked the man down.

At his next session, he was storming, demanding, and belligerent. He insisted he did not have a real friend in the world except the analyst, and that the analyst was paid to be friendly. He felt that he stood alone against the world but was "ready for them." Again he demanded sedatives to ease his tension and was given some after the hour ended.

Following this session he walked about the grounds, played records on a phonograph in one of the lounges, went to his room, got out his bathrobe belt and tried to hang himself in the bathroom. Within a few moments he was found, cut down, and revived with artificial respiration and stimulants.

Dr. Knight went to see him in his room. He had a severe rope burn on his neck. He expressed resentment at having been rescued. He said he had played over and over on the phonograph one popular song before he tried to hang himself. The song was "You Leave Me Breathless." While listening to the music, he had fantasies of both older women and younger girls with their arms around his neck embracing him. He said he felt one moment of extreme peace just before he lost consciousness.

Dr. Knight saw him in his room for several days. As they talked the young man recalled a previous suicide attempt which he had made at home after his breakdown at college. He had taken his loaded .45 revolver, put it to his temple, and pulled the trigger. It merely clicked. He examined it, found it fully loaded, and was so unnerved that he could not try it again. He walked for two hours, telling no one of his attempt to kill himself. He said he felt as if he were now doubly living on borrowed time and that the next attempt would surely succeed.

After he recovered, for the following few days, he was depressed, tense, and provocative. He raged at the previous patient in Dr. Knight's office because he found the couch still warm. He called this patient a sissy and a pervert, and verbally attacked other patients who seemed effeminate to him.

He described a dream in which a fish spoke to him and invited him to kiss it on the mouth. He debated whether or not to do so, then awoke. In associating to this dream, after an obvious struggle with himself, he confessed he had lied about his reactions to homosexuals. He had not knocked them all down. There had been several homosexual episodes in boyhood about which he felt great anxiety and remorse. He related the details of these experiences.

This was the seventy-fifth hour of the analysis and proved to be a turning point, according to Dr. Knight. The young man could finally begin to face his passive sexual wishes toward men. He admitted that for a long time he had been aware of the connection between his belligerency and his determination not to admit the earlier erotic experiences with men.

Some weeks later he confessed he had passive sexual fantasies and wishes in relation to Dr. Knight. To fight these, the young man took flight into heterosexuality. He spent hours every day and evening with a girl friend at the sanatorium. It was not until after she left for a vacation that he realized, he said, the truth of what Dr. Knight had been pointing out—he was seeking affection and protection from the girl friend that he really wished to obtain from a man, specifically, his analyst.

He admitted fantasies in which the analyst attempted to seduce him. These had been followed by fantasies of intimidating the analyst with a gun. One day he had stood in front of a local pawnshop window admiring a revolver and pictured himself buying it, loading it, and taking it to the analytic hour. He saw himself sitting in the chair instead of lying on the couch, and twirling the gun around his finger while he informed Dr. Knight that he had only a few more minutes to live. He would then sit and watch the analyst quail and squirm. But, the more he thought about it, the more he became afraid that Dr. Knight would not be intimidated. It was then he saw the connection between his passive homosexual wishes and the need to intimidate the man toward whom the passive wishes were directed. (The attack on the man was both a substitute for the sexual act and a protection against its taking place.)

In following sessions, the young man expressed deep feelings of resentment and jealousy toward the analyst's other patients; then toward his own brother. He came eagerly to his appointments and, according to Dr. Knight, produced "a wealth of memories and fantasies."

His tension disappeared and he said that he wanted to live, not die, feeling there was much happiness and productiveness ahead of him.

Now instead of bragging about his fighting, he talked of himself as a coward and weakling. He admitted that his report of hundreds of fights in which he had knocked down other men were largely false. He said he was really frightened of the idea of fighting and had taken part in very few fights.

After fourteen months of treatment he was able to return to college, where, according to Dr. Knight, he showed considerable capacity for sustained, conscientious work. He made a number of friends, was graduated with honors, and went to work in an engineering firm where he was given a responsible position.

In summing up, Dr. Knight pointed out that the analysis had resulted in the loss of this young man's symptoms of aggressiveness and arrogance. Instead of fantasies of killing people with machine guns and seeing enemies lurking everywhere, he now felt he wanted friendship from men and love from a woman.

The task in the analysis of such a patient is to uncover the fears that drive him to his aggressive attitude and then to analyze these fears and insecurities, Dr. Knight pointed out. When this is done, the person's strong need for love becomes conscious and can be accepted by him.

# Less Immoral Than Murder

One of the strongest impulses is the desire to kill when one feels threatened either physically or psychologically. A person needs such an impulse in order to survive, to save his own life should he be attacked.

If someone's early life, emotionally speaking, has been terrifying, this impulse, if denied, may become diverted in later years into channels that are destructive to him. For only when a man is able to face the previously unknown causes of his terror can he free himself from their tyranny and tackle the meaningful problems of life, no longer wasting energy on the ghosts of the past.

The following case history, written by Dr. Ludwig Eidelberg, shows how one man tried to hide his murderous impulses from himself. It was originally entitled "A Bottle Broke" when it appeared in *Take Off Your Mask* (published by Pyramid Books in 1948). Dr. Eidelberg illustrates how repressed hatred may erupt in the form of an obsessional act in which a person tries unsuccessfully to deny his conflicts.

Although the following reads as though it occurred in one hour, Dr. Eidelberg has condensed into one session material obtained in daily psychoanalytic sessions that took place over a period of eight months.

"There are many hours in which nothing happens," he writes in the introduction to his book, "and you (the reader) would become bored or discouraged if I tried to explain in detail how complicated *real* analytical work is. To make these stories readable, I have had to omit, modify, condense and blend together many of the facts I have collected."

¶A man about thirty years old, thin, with a dark complexion and needing a shave, came to see Dr. Eidelberg. The patient was sloppily dressed, although his clothes were of good quality. His wrinkled tie was carelessly knotted.

When Dr. Eidelberg indicated that the man, whose name was Mr. Lowe, sit in the armchair beside the desk, he walked toward it, his body bent slightly forward and his arms held rigidly away from his sides. As he sat down, he held his hands in the air so they would not touch anything, then lowered them, and hung them over the padded arms of the chair.

Dr. Eidelberg asked Mr. Lowe why he had come. He replied, his hands twitching, "I'm here because of glass. I mean, little pieces of glass in my hands." He had a slight lisp.

"What do you mean by 'glass in your hands'?" asked Dr. Eidelberg.

"These pieces—I'm afraid that the tiny pieces of glass I have in my hands will injure anyone I shake hands with, or touch when I pass 'em," he explained. "I—I'm careful not to come near anybody. I watch myself closely, but the fear remains."

He held up his hands to show Dr. Eidelberg the "little pieces of glass."

"Do you see the little pieces of glass, Mr. Lowe?" asked Dr. Eidelberg.

He fidgeted in the chair. "No, I don't. The pieces in the ends of my fingers are so small that nobody can see 'em. But they're still there."

"Are you sure they're there?"

"Of course I'm not!" he replied. "How can anybody be sure of anything?"

He went on to say that at times he felt as though the pieces had disappeared and he once again felt free. He said that when his sister examined his hands and told him they were clean, he would feel "good" for a few minutes, but shortly the doubts and fears again returned. They were so strong, he had been unable to work.

He said, "I just can't! I'm too scared. You may think I'm silly, but I am scared!"

Dr. Eidelberg asked how long he had been possessed by these doubts and fears. He said about two years, during which time he had seen many doctors, none of whom had been able to help him. Finally one sent him to Dr. Eidelberg, thinking psychoanalysis might uncover the root of his fears.

Encouraged by Dr. Eidelberg to talk freely, Mr. Lowe told something of his background. He had been the manager of a small candy factory that he had inherited from his father. Mr. Lowe and his brother-in-law, Harold, took over operation of the factory when Mr. Lowe's father died.

He then recalled a particular day, two years before, saying, "One day—let's see, it was July thirty-first, a very hot day—my family went away for the summer. By family, I mean my sister Edith and my brother-in-law Harold."

He told how he had stayed behind to take care of the factory. That was when his fears first started. He went to the laboratory to get a bottle of coloring fluid for the candy, opened the cabinet where it was kept, and suddenly noticed that his arm was trembling. He tried to put the bottle down on the table. He could not reach the table, yet could not keep his fingers closed. They felt paralyzed. The bottle fell to the floor, smashing into a thousand pieces.

"I tried to clean up the mess," he said, "but I was scared of hurting my hands with some pieces of glass. I forced myself to do it, and finally I was through. Then I washed my hands carefully, to get rid of any pieces of glass that might've remained. I spent nearly an hour on it, but I still had the idea that some glass was sticking to them."

Dr. Eidelberg asked if he had ever broken a bottle before. Mr. Lowe recalled he had broken one just the day before, while working late in the laboratory. His brother-in-law was present and scolded him for his carelessness. He ordered Mr. Lowe to clean up the laboratory carefully in order to avoid another accident.

"What kind of accident?" asked Dr. Eidelberg.

Mr. Lowe was silent for a few moments. Then he said, "Well—a piece of glass could get into the candy. Somebody could swallow it, and die!"

"Where did you ever get such a fantastic idea?" asked Dr. Eidelberg.

Mr. Lowe insisted it was not fantastic at all. He said that their competitor, a Mr. Molts, had been warned several times by the authorities, then fined, and finally put in jail for a year after they found nails in his candy. Mr. Lowe admitted that he had been pleased when Mr. Molts's factory had to close because it meant more business for his own.

But he had pitied the son, young Molts, a friend of his. He felt the son had been badly treated by the elder Molts, who underpaid him and ordered him to do hard work in the factory. He said of the father, "The old bastard was a real tyrant."

So he offered young Molts a job in his factory, which the boy accepted. But not long after, Mr. Lowe had to fire him because young Molts started to arrive late—first a half hour, then a whole hour, then two, three, and four hours. At first Mr. Lowe kept warning him, and although he promised to be on time, he never kept his promise.

"And then he got me sore by inventing a foolish story as an excuse," he said. "He told me that whenever he touched someone on the way to the factory, he had to go home right away and wash his hands, to prevent the person he'd touched from dying! He wanted me to believe that he could bring death to any man he touched!"

He went on, "But this idea that he could kill a man just by touching him was screwy. And you know—he really believed it! He refused to touch me, and he got panicky when I tried to touch him. He used to hurry out of the office."

Mr. Lowe then asked Dr. Eidelberg, "What would you have told him to make him give up his screwy ideas?"

Dr. Eidelberg replied, "I would have attempted to find out how he got his ideas. For instance, whether he felt satisfied with the new job at your factory . . . Whether he felt that it was right for his father's factory to be closed and the old gentleman in jail. You say his father treated him rather badly?"

Mr. Lowe shrugged. "Still, it was his own father."

"Yes, his own father—someone he admired. Someone he loved, even if he had good reason to hate him, to wish him evil and to rejoice when he was punished. Someone who had taken care of him when he was a little boy, who played with him—had given him toys. Someone who taught him to control his own desires, and to obey when he gave orders. Somebody so powerful that he may have been afraid to offend him by a rebellious thought," said Dr. Eidelberg.

Whereupon Mr. Lowe asked in surprise, "How the hell are you able to describe him so well, when you never met him?"

"Because I've met many like him. In spite of our differences, all of us have many things in common."

At which Mr. Lowe admitted, "Yes, Doc—when you described my friend so well, I was reminded of the way I felt about my father. I was also afraid of my thoughts, and couldn't stop them." He shuddered. "Evil thoughts, vicious thoughts, which come—and go . . ." He became lost in recollection, and then he said, "Yes, they make you feel guilty, all right—as if you wanted the bad things to happen."

He was silent again. Dr. Eidelberg said, "Such as—when the Molts factory closed. Your friend, young Molts, may have had all sorts of hostile wishes about his father—perhaps he even felt that it served him right! Perhaps he had the impression that his father's punishment was a judgment upon him for what he had done to his son. Young Molts may have regarded the punishment as a revenge he was able to take upon his father, and he could have treated the whole incident as a fulfillment of his own hostile wishes. In other words, perhaps it appeared to him as if his hostile thoughts had the power to act without his own volition, as if he were a magician who, by a curse, could destroy his enemy."

Mr. Lowe mumbled, "How often I wished I had that power. . . ." Then he asked hastily, "Wouldn't you?"

"I really don't know," said Dr. Eidelberg. "You see, we all would like to have more power than we do—but more power means more responsibility. If I were angry at someone, and wished something bad to happen to him, I'd be terribly shocked if my wish were fulfilled. I think I'd be scared to have such a terrible weapon in my possession—a thought that could kill! I'm afraid it would kill all my thoughts. I prefer to achieve my goals by my actions."

He explained further that young Molts could not enjoy either his freedom from his father or his better job with Mr. Lowe, because to him it meant the satisfaction of a hostility he had carried from childhood toward his father. Dr. Eidelberg pointed out that young Molts's need to wash his hands, and his fear he might kill someone by touching them, was connected with his unconscious hatred of his father, one he had never admitted to himself.

Dr. Eidelberg asked Mr. Lowe, at one point, if he liked Harold, his brother-in-law. Mr. Lowe replied, "Who, Harold? Sure I do. In a way. Well," he added lamely, "I think I do."

Dr. Eidelberg asked, "Have you ever quarreled with him?"

"Oh, I suppose I have."

"About what?"

"Mostly about the factory. You see, when Harold married my sister, he wanted to be a teacher. But when my father died, he decided that, since he was the oldest in the family, he ought to become the head of our firm. My mother thought he was right, so that's how he got to be my boss. I don't want you to get the wrong idea about him. He's really a fine guy. He's smart, has read many books—he's a regular bookworm—but he knows practically nothing about candy. Still, being the boss, he gives the orders—and they often make no sense."

"Yet in spite of this, you like him?"

Mr. Lowe shrugged. "You can't hate your own brother-in-law."

"I would, if he tried to interfere with my work."

"What use would that be? You couldn't send him away, could you?"

"I don't know what I could do, but I'd certainly hate him."

"And make your sister and your whole family unhappy?"

"Ah, I didn't say that I'd express my hatred!"

"You mean you'd keep it a secret?"

"I might."

"But why?"

"Well, perhaps to avoid hurting the family. Don't misunderstand me. When I said that I would hate my brother-in-law, I meant that he would have provoked that hatred in me."

"What's the use of feelings you can't talk about?"

"A feeling doesn't have to have a purpose. It is aroused in us by certain events or people, and we have little control over it. However, we're usually able to control its expression."

"But isn't it terribly hard to control yourself?"

"Sometimes it is. Still, the only other way is to repress a hostile feeling."

"What do you mean by 'repress'?"

"Repression is a mechanism which enables us not to feel an embarrassing emotion."

Mr. Lowe ran his fingers through his hair. "How can that be done?"

"Oh, there are many ways to avoid facing unpleasant emotions. For instance, in order to hide fear from yourself, you may try to laugh it off. Or, to deny that you like someone, you may look for something which would make you hate him. Or you may try to like and to hate at the same time, without making up your mind. This last mixture of positive and negative emotions would be useful in keeping the original emotion away from your conscious mind."

"I thought that I liked and disliked Harold because he's part nice, and part nasty. Now if I'm to believe you, I really hated him."

"I didn't say really! I said 'unconsciously,'" explained Dr. Eidelberg.

Mr. Lowe clasped and unclasped his hands. "What does 'unconscious' mean?" he asked.

"It means that there is hatred in you without your being aware of it. And you're not aware of it because it's hidden behind a mask, one that shows you both liking and disliking Harold."

"But who made the mask? I'm sure I didn't!"

"The mask was also produced by an unconscious part of you. You behave like a rich man who gets all sorts of unpleasant letters, and who hires a secretary, not only to avoid knowing their contents, but also not to have to deal with them. The secretary opens the letters, reads them, and answers them, without her boss being bothered."

"Am I supposed to have that kind of a secretary?"

"You are."

"I like that idea. It's sort of practical," Mr. Lowe said.

"But very expensive," said Dr. Eidelberg.

"What d'you mean? Do I have to pay for it?"

"You do. As you can imagine, a secretary who has so much power, and so little knowledge, may make many mistakes. Our unconscious is a helpful institution, as long as it's under the control of our conscious mind. It may shock you to discover that you hate Harold, but after having discovered it, you'll be able to find some way of dealing with it."

"For instance?"

"Well, you could persuade him and your mother that he ought to resign as head of the factory."

Mr. Lowe was shocked. "Oh, I couldn't do that!"

"After finding out more about your hatred, you probably could," said Dr. Eidelberg.

Mr. Lowe's hands shook as he took a handkerchief from his pocket and wiped his perspiring face. "But isn't it immoral to try to kick out your brother-in-law?" he asked. "What about my conscience?"

"Well, I think that persuading him to resign is less immoral than putting glass into candy," said Dr. Eidelberg.

Mr. Lowe suddenly sat erect and his mouth dropped open. "Are you saying that—that I wanted to put pieces of glass into the candy so that Harold would be arrested?"

"Certainly not, or you wouldn't be here, suffering from the fear that such a thing could happen. Not you, but your unconscious wanted to attempt it."

Mr. Lowe put his hand to his forehead. "But I had no idea that a part of me is so cruel!" Then he said, as if in extenuation of himself, "But I never tried to *do* anything! They were just thoughts!"

"What do you mean by 'just thoughts'? True, a mere thought won't injure another person, but aggressive thoughts will, in the long run, influence your behavior in many ways."

The session was about over. Dr. Eidelberg asked Mr. Lowe to let him know if he wanted to return to start intensive treatment. Mr. Lowe said he thought he did, but first he wanted to talk it over with his sister, and he would telephone Dr. Eidelberg that afternoon. Still bending forward from his waist and holding his hands rigidly away from his body, Mr. Lowe went to the door, opened it, then closed it cautiously behind him.

¶Mr. Lowe did return. He saw Dr. Eidelberg for eight months, at the end of which time he no longer had the obsession that he had pieces of glass in his fingers. Dr. Eidelberg helped him to realize how this symptom had satisfied his hostility against Harold. Harold, the interloper, the man whom Mr. Lowe's own mother had put in charge over her son, now had to take care of the factory by himself. Mr. Lowe arranged it so that, because of his fear, his sister had to accompany him wherever he went (she had even waited for him in the reception room while he saw Dr. Eidelberg), which would also make Harold's life more difficult. Mr. Lowe was unconsciously hurting Harold, his sister, and himself—his work had been one of his chief sources of pleasure, and he had cut himself off from it.

Mr. Lowe also recognized that this apparent inability to make up his mind was not the result of the complexity of the problem, but of his unconscious unwillingness to choose one attitude and give up the other. He couldn't continue to fight and appease Harold at the same time. He had to decide whether he wanted to continue to work with Harold, even though it would mean a great deal of humiliation, or to work without him, although that would mean offending the family.

His neurosis had allowed him to avoid the ultimate decision. By becoming ill, he was unable to work, and his family had had to take care of him and pay for his treatment. In this way he was able to punish them without openly expressing his hostility. At the same time, by punishing himself, he avoided feelings of guilt.

The fact that by keeping his symptom he could satisfy both his love and his hatred and didn't have to make a decision as to which triumphed had been one of the advantages of his illness. Dr. Eidelberg suggested to Mr. Lowe that his method of dealing with his unconscious wishes was, in the long run, far too expensive, psychically speaking. As he came to understand his unconscious wishes, he could take responsibility for his decisions. By obtaining more control over his unconscious, learning its language, and helping it work *for* him, instead of against him, Dr. Eidelberg noted, the young man would undoubtedly be able to have a happier life.

# "I Love You So Much I Must Kill You"

Today many teen-agers, including juvenile delinquents, are receiving treatment. This not only saves the adolescent much anguish but also benefits society, which pays a costly price for the destructive behavior of many of its young people.

In the following case, Dr. Hyman Spotnitz, psychoanalyst, Leo Nagelberg, psychologist, and Yonata Feldman, psychiatric social worker, describe how they helped a thirteen-year-old boy with extremely destructive feelings to understand his deeper conflicts. Mr. Nagelberg was the therapist and Dr. Spotnitz and Mrs. Feldman served as consultants.

The boy was one of five schizophrenic children selected for individual treatment as part of a research project at the Child Guidance Institute of the Jewish Board of Guardians, New York. [The first paper describing his treatment appeared in *The American Journal of Orthopsychiatry*, Vol. XXVI, No. 1 (January 1956). A more detailed description will appear in a yet unpublished book, *The Withdrawn Child*, by Dr. Spotnitz, Mr. Nagelberg and Mrs. Feldman.]

This case shows how a child can turn his hatred inward and destroy himself psychologically to protect a parent from his uncontrolled and potentially murderous feelings.

¶At the age of thirteen, Harry was brought to the Jewish Board of Guardians by his mother, who was afraid he might kill her. He had physically attacked her several times, and once he had threatened her with a knife, then jumped on her in bed, thrown a pillow over her face, and tried to choke her.

"I love you so much I must kill you," he told her.

He accused her of not loving him. He resented any time she spent away from him, even with her own mother. He would hide her clothing so she could not dress to go out.

Harry was an extremely withdrawn boy. He had no friends; after school, he would come home and refuse to leave the house. He would often lie in bed all day, listening to the radio with the covers pulled over him.

His mother told the social worker that her son's peculiar behavior started after the death of his father, when the boy was five. She and Harry then went to live with his grandmother for two years. It was at this time Harry's difficulties became pronounced. She now worked, and lived alone with the boy.

When the therapist telephoned Harry, asking him to come for an interview, Harry said, "I will not," and banged down the telephone receiver. But his mother brought him to the therapist's office, and remained in the reception room during the session.

Harry asked, in a low, tense voice, if he *had* to come for help. The therapist told him he did not have to. (According to the authors, if the therapist acted as if he did not care whether Harry came or not, the boy would then feel free to come. "Psychological reflection of the indifferent attitude of the child is understood by the child to be a duplication of his attitude; he experiences it as indicating liking and interest," they maintained.)

Then, in the same monotone, Harry asked if he could come just once or twice. The therapist said he could. When Harry was given a date for his second visit, he announced he was not going to show up. Then he changed his mind and said he would. He grudgingly admitted he thought it was a privilege to get help. But he could not understand, he said, why the therapist did not *make* him show up.

In the second interview, he asked the therapist what he was supposed to do. He was told to speak about his life. He asked whether the therapist was going to help him. The therapist said he was there to "understand" him so that Harry could understand himself better. Harry then started to talk about his schoolwork, his interests, the books he read.

At the third session, the boy announced he had nothing important to say. The therapist kept silent. Harry then talked about some of his experiences. He admitted he liked to talk, and he was grateful that someone was listening.

Just before the fourth interview, Harry's mother telephoned to complain that he had again threatened to kill her. When Harry arrived, the therapist told him his mother had called. The boy said nothing for twenty-five minutes, and then asked what his mother had said. The therapist did not answer. Harry was silent another twelve minutes before he repeated that he wanted to know exactly what his mother said. Still the therapist said nothing.

Harry asked whether the therapist was going to say a word. The therapist indicated that Harry should talk. The boy asked why the therapist smoked, since smoking caused cancer, and wanted to know how, if the therapist did not have self-control, could he control other people? At the end of this session, Harry seemed reluctant to leave.

When the fifth interview started, Harry sat in silence. The therapist waited. Then Harry asked if the therapist could suggest something to discuss.

"Why?" asked the therapist.

"Because we could exchange ideas, and I could find out about you," said the boy. (Here he was giving up some of what the authors call his "pathological narcissism" and evidencing interest in another person.)

The therapist kept quiet. Harry then talked about the war in Korea.

Harry now came regularly for interviews, and gradually started to talk about himself and about his feelings for his mother and his dead father. He admitted that he cried at times because he felt nobody loved him. He preferred staying home to going out because no one understood him or liked him, he said.

During the fourteenth interview he remarked, "If only mother would not take me so seriously!" He complained that she wanted him to go out, but he liked to read and practice the clarinet. She would interrupt him to run errands for her and he disliked doing them, he said.

At the twenty-second interview Harry made the suggestion that his mother undergo treatment, to which the therapist agreed. (Here, again, the boy was starting to think of others.) During the thirtieth interview he expressed the hope that his mother, after she had seen a therapist, would "get off" all the bad things about him, and then tell the therapist all the things she loved about him.

At the thirty-fourth interview Harry discussed an early homosexual experience. During the next interview he said he had instructed himself to be "normal" for a week, and that to be normal meant to be like everybody else. He added, "To be normal also means to say anything that comes into your mind."

At the next session he expressed the wish that his mother would not "push" him so much. (He was starting to realize how much benefit he was getting from the therapist, who would not "push" at all and who allowed him to make up his own mind.)

During the forty-second interview Harry said that now when he fought with his mother he watched himself fighting, as though he were another person. He said that since he regarded the other person as "silly," he found himself "silly," so he stopped fighting with her.

At the sixty-sixth interview Harry told the therapist that he wished he could behave as the therapist did, with the same amount of self-understanding and control. Three interviews later he was expressing an opposite opinion, saying that the therapist was "a logical piece of machinery and didn't show too much feeling." Harry said that he did not want to show or say too much, or confess he needed or liked another person.

The therapist asked, "What is wrong about showing that one likes or needs another person?"

"Now we're getting somewhere," Harry answered. "I have an idea that we always move very slowly. I finally get the idea that you are driving at. You would not mind if I feel toward you as if you were my father."

Then some of his deeper feelings about his dead father came out. He went on to say that he was always afraid of expressing feelings of love for his father because they might be homosexual. He said he remembered he only got love from his father, but that even as a small child, he hated his father because he was a rival for his mother. He spoke of an electric train his father had given him and said he felt he had not deserved it because he hated his father so much and imagined that his father hated him in return.

He admitted that he was glad his father was dead, because now he had his mother all to himself. After his father's death, he had hated all men. He didn't want his mother to remarry. He had the idea that men hate one another; he could not believe that a father could love a son, or a brother, a brother. But now, he said, he saw that he had been wrong. It was possible for a father and son to love each other without being accused of homosexuality.

During previous sessions Harry had discussed his fears about masturbation, saying that he worried about this. The therapist had encouraged him to worry. At his 105th interview, Harry talked about his feelings of depression. Now he spoke of his desire to kill himself, and the murderous wishes that rose up in him when he felt that his mother, others in his family, or the therapist did not measure up to his ideal of them. He said that when he felt he was not loved, even by himself, he would become depressed and wonder what was the use of being alive, and think of killing himself. The therapist asked why he had not killed himself. (According to the authors, had the therapist encouraged Harry to stay alive, this would have pushed back his desire to kill himself, whereas being asked why he did not kill himself, left him free to re-examine the whole question of whether he should, or should not, kill himself.) Harry admitted that the response given him—a response which obviously could be voiced only in the proper context and after the establishment of a healthy emotional relationship—made him feel that it would be better to try to work out his own problems than to commit suicide. He expressed himself in similar fashion about the discussion of his fears of being insane, or being watched, or being a freak, a sex maniac, and a homosexual.

"When you come for treatment, you put your worries into words and unload them on the therapist," Harry said. "I like other people to do the worrying for me, but then again I don't like it because you remain indebted and won't be free. I used to think you didn't want me to worry about masturbation, so a load was taken off my mind when *I thought I had the right to worry*. Then I stopped worrying." He added that he thought being human meant "to be imperfect, to worry, to be responsible, and to be free."

Harry remarked, during this session, that it had become easier for him to talk about his thoughts. He said, "I learned that it is all right to talk crazily without having to act crazily. Now it seems strange that I once felt watched and talked about by people. If you can admit to yourself that it may be all right to have all sorts of crazy impulses, it is easier to control them, and they no longer bother you."

He also said that, at first, he had expected the therapist to be "perfect," and it hurt him when his "illusions were broken." He added, "But it also made me more alive, and you became more human. You mixed me up, but it is comforting to talk to you. We have a common meeting ground, and I have a chance to be like you. If I can think that you may have faults, it is easier to talk about my own."

He disclosed his feelings about some of the therapist's prohibitions. He said that he had both liked and resented being told not to masturbate, not to threaten his mother, and not to peep at women undressing. He had wanted, yet had not wanted, to be told to stop committing these acts. "I knew that eventually I had to stop those activities, and I felt that you were trying to help me stop," he said. (The authors noted that the therapist's directions had been given not for their effect outside the session, but for their immediate stimulating effect during the interview.)

At one point Harry yearned to be adopted by the therapist and his wife. He became depressed when he realized this was impossible, and then he said, "I decided that the best way for me to be loved was to be working with you in our therapy."

Harry at times discussed the theme of understanding one's self in a repetitious way. The therapist asked him why he did so. The boy replied that he always hammered away at one problem at a time. He said, "It is like shutting myself up in a back room and shutting out everything else. I hammer away and it is like grabbing for some security, and also justifying myself that I am right." (The authors commented that this was an illustration of how some very emotionally ill children attempt to "insulate" themselves against their feelings and acts by five different methods: self-insulation, shutting out stimuli, forceful repetition as a protective pattern, clinging, and self-justification.)

One day Harry said he would like to talk to the therapist twenty-four hours a day, and then he would feel satisfied. The therapist replied, "I am not supposed to satisfy you."

"You are doing a good job not to satisfy me," said the boy.

The therapist pointed out that one had to learn to take frustration in living, and that therapy was helpful because it enabled a person to adjust himself to frustrating situations. Harry said he realized this. He commented, "It is not good to live in fantasy."

At the 154th interview Harry told the therapist that he formerly felt tense and fearful when he had to speak to people, but now he could speak freely because he was no longer "mad at them" and no longer felt they were "mad" at him. He said that he used to hold back thoughts from the therapist, wondering if it would "pay off" to disclose them, but now he said everything that came to his mind, even if it did not "pay off." He said he felt the therapist liked him, and so he could talk freely.

During the 167th interview Harry commented that instead of taking over the feelings of other people, it would be better for him to follow his own. If he felt his own feelings first, he said, it would be easier to understand what others were feeling.

After three years of treatment, Harry started to stay at school after hours and join clubs and to make friends freely. His temper tantrums disappeared. He took out girls, although he said he did not feel too comfortable with them yet.

His mother, who when she first brought him to the agency

feared that he would have to be put in a mental hospital, was delighted with her son's change as he began to take an interest in the world around him. He was more direct and outspoken, and seemed much more self-confident.

Harry has since kept in touch with his therapist and reported his scholastic progress. Recently he was graduated from medical school and is now about to begin his medical career.

In summing up the case of Harry and the four other schizophrenic children who were treated at the agency, the authors pointed out that each child improved by gaining sufficient confidence in himself and the therapist, so that he could speak of whatever he felt, no matter how embarrassing or shameful he believed it to be. The therapist provides the protective barrier the child never had, so that the child can "play out, feel and eventually verbalize his destructive impulses. This has the effect of increasing his tolerance to frustration."

In Harry's case, while his father lived, the latter stood as a barrier to the boy's natural feelings of wanting to possess his mother. But upon the death of his father, there was no one to say nay to Harry's strong impulses. He did not know what to do with his unleashed, uncontrolled emotions toward his mother. Instead of giving in to the erotic desires, Harry fought his wishes with hatred.

Then he fought his hate, which he could control most of the time, by turning it inward onto himself. He was, in the authors' words, "willing to destroy his own ego by psychological or physical suicide to protect his parent from his uncontrolled aggressiveness."

Harry and the other children were helped by the therapist, first to express hatred, then to feel it, understand it, and control it. Subsequently they were able to experience feelings of love for the therapist and for themselves.

# Erna's Envy

Psychological help given to little children before their emotional illness becomes too severe is another province in which psychoanalysis has shown success. At first, many did not believe children could be helped, but pioneers such as Anna Freud and the late Melanie Klein proved they could be.

In the following case, Mrs. Klein describes a little girl who was unable to tame her anger, had a poor image of her body, and went through much difficulty trying to relate to people. Her mother's apparent emotional illness meant that, instead of being protective of her daughter, she could not help her guard against her anxiety.

All children have fantasies but it is only when the child is possessed by such intense fear and anger that his fantasies control him, rather than he controlling them, that the child becomes disturbed.

Mrs. Klein demonstrated once again the significance of Freud's distinction between "psychic reality," the unconscious and conscious fantasies that may govern a person, and "reality," the world as most men see it. She also developed several theories of her own, some of which have been controversial among psychoanalysts. She believed, for instance, that the desire of the child to possess the parent of the opposite sex exists as early as the second half of the first year of life. It is then, she held, that the child starts to modify his raw, primitive impulses and build a conscience, and this is the start of the Oedipal conflict.

Mrs. Klein stressed the tragic effect on a child of separation from the mother. She looked with sympathy and understanding upon the struggle of children to become civilized. She wrote, ". . . . even in their earliest years children not only experience sexual impulses and anxiety, but undergo great disillusionments. Along with the belief in the asexuality of the child has perished the belief in the 'Paradise of Childhood.' "

In her treatment of the very young child Mrs. Klein used a technique called play analysis. Through play and games in Mrs. Klein's office, the child expressed his fantasies, wishes, and actual experiences in a symbolic way. He often made use of the same archaic and primitive modes of expression as appear in dreams, she said. A single toy or a single bit of action in play might hold many different meanings, as in the following case of Erna.

Titled "An Obsessional Neurosis in a Six-Year-Old Girl," it first appeared as a chapter in her book *The Psychoanalysis of Children.* (The third edition was published by Grove Press in 1960. The first edition was published by Hogarth Press, London, in 1932.)

In this case Mrs. Klein shows how the fantasies of a very disturbed little girl can become so intense and powerful that they hamper a child's learning as well as her sexual development. Erna's fantasies served as a protection against a world she felt to be dangerous. She had been an exceptionally frightened and angry baby who, as Mrs. Klein points out, "never got over her weaning." Her anger was not eased, according to Mrs. Klein, when she was permitted, as a child, to witness her mother and father in the act of sexual intercourse.

¶When Erna came to Mrs. Klein's office, she was six years old, an only child who suffered from some severe symptoms. She could not sleep at night because she feared robbers would break into her room. She would lie on her face and endlessly bang her head on the pillow, or she would make a rocking movement during which she sat or lay on her back. She sucked her thumb continuously. She masturbated excessively, often in front of strangers, and almost all the time at kindergarten.

She was a very depressed little girl. She told Mrs. Klein, "There's something I don't like about life." At times she showered her mother with affection; then she would become very angry and throw temper tantrums. She completely dominated her mother, who said of her, "She swallows me up."

Erna was too disturbed to remain in school, even though she

was very bright. Soon after her analysis was started she entered first grade, but it became evident she was incapable of absorbing facts in the classroom. She could not adapt either to her teachers or to the other pupils. It took her two years to master what most children learned in a few months.

Mrs. Klein described Erna thus: "Obsessive brooding and a curiously unchildlike nature were depicted in the suffering look upon the little girl's face." Mrs. Klein noted that photographs of her at the age of three showed the same neurotic, worried look.

Erna "made an impression of being unusually precocious sexually," Mrs. Klein said, adding that the child's unusual sexual precocity seemed to strike everyone around her. She was very provocative with men and boys. When Erna was between six and nine months old, her mother had noticed with what evident sexual pleasure she responded to the care of her body, especially to the cleansing of her genitals and anus. Her mother then used greater discretion in washing her daughter, but the child, "who had looked upon the earlier and more elaborate attention as a form of seduction, felt this later reticence as a frustration," Mrs. Klein explained.

"This feeling of being seduced, behind which there lay a desire to be seduced, was constantly being repeated all through her life. In every relationship, e.g., to her nurse and the other people who brought her up and also in her analysis, she tried to repeat the situation of being seduced or alternately to bring forward the charge that she was being seduced."

Very early in life, Erna appeared to be in emotional trouble. By the time she was two and a half, she was unmanageable. Yet it was not until she was four that her masturbatory habits in public and her obsessive thumb sucking and sleeplessness began to disturb her parents. And they did not bring her to Mrs. Klein for help until she was six.

"The fact that she herself felt that she was ill—at the very beginning of her treatment she begged me to help her—was of great assistance to me in analyzing her," Mrs. Klein said.

In her first session Erna noticed a small carriage which sat on a little table among other toys. She pushed it toward Mrs. Klein and said she had come to fetch her, but instead she placed a toy woman in it, then added a toy man. She made the two figures kiss one another as they drove up and down in the carriage. Then she placed another toy man in a second carriage, and had him collide with the couple, run over them, and kill them. Then she had him roast them and eat them.

Another time in her play the attacking toy man was hurled to the ground, but the woman helped him up, comforted him, and got a divorce from her husband to marry him. In still another scene, Erna put the original toy man and woman in a house which they defended against a burglar, but the burglar, slipping inside, set the house afire, and it burned down while the man and woman burst into flames. The burglar was left unharmed.

The third person—the little toy man (and the burglar)—apparently represented Erna in her fantasies, while the original toy woman and man were her mother and father. Erna's play, according to Mrs. Klein, revealed some of her deeper wishes. She wanted to get rid of her father, as shown by her mother divorcing him to marry the second man (herself). She also wished to destroy both her mother and father by roasting and eating them.

Erna sometimes played the role of her mother as she acted out scenes, ordering Mrs. Klein to be the child. She would give Mrs. Klein a toy engine to put into her mouth, saying, as she admired its two red gilded lamps, "They're so lovely, all red and burning." Then she would snatch the engine from Mrs. Klein, put the two lamps into her own mouth, and suck them. These games were invariably followed by outbreaks of rage, envy, and aggressive acts that, in turn, were succeeded by remorse and attempts on Erna's part to placate her analyst.

Erna's hatred for her mother came out in many ways. She threw the toy woman into prison where she starved to death, or the toy woman was seized with an illness of which Erna said, "God has spoken to her," whereupon the child fell sick with something called "mother's agitation" and died of it. As a result, the father killed the mother as punishment. Then the child was brought back to life, and the father married her. The mother also was restored to the living, but was turned into a child by the father with the help of his magic wand and thereafter, as punishment, had to suffer all the scorn and ill treatment she had inflicted on the child. Here Erna was repeating in fantasy what she felt her mother had done to her, by expressing what she would like to do to her mother if the roles were reversed.

Another time Erna remarked that everything in the room had been turned into feces and that it was her mother's fault, and she hurled her mother into prison. She cleaned up the dirt her mother had caused, calling herself "Mrs. Dirt Parade." She thus won the admiration and love of her father for her cleanliness, and he married her and allowed her to do all the cooking.

At home Erna felt extremely persecuted by her mother and felt she had to watch her all the time. She also felt responsible for every illness her mother suffered. According to Mrs. Klein, she unconsciously expected a corresponding punishment because she believed she had caused the illness out of her deep desire to kill her mother.

"Her whole relationship to her mother had been distorted by [her angry feelings]," said Mrs. Klein. "Every educational measure, every act of nursery discipline, every unavoidable frustration, was felt by her as a purely sadistic act on the part of her mother, done with a view of humiliating and ill-treating her."

When Erna played the mother in her make-believe world, she showed affection to her toy child only when it represented a baby. Then she would nurse and wash it, be tender to it, and even forgive it when it became dirty. This she did, because she felt she had been treated lovingly only as long as she was an infant. Erna treated her older toy-child cruelly, allowing it to be tortured in various ways by devils, and in the end killed.

Once, after being brutal to her older "child," she asked Mrs. Klein in a deeply moved voice, "Should I *really* have treated my children like that?" This was when she was starting to become conscious of her hatred for her mother. She was beginning to see her more as a real person rather than through a haze of angry fantasies.

Although Erna was an only child, she had many fantasies about the arrival of brothers and sisters. Her occasional wish for a brother or sister was determined by a number of motives, Mrs. Klein found. She desired a child of her own. She also wanted someone who would be her ally against whom she considered her terrifying parents.

Mrs. Klein noted that, from her experience, the only child suffers to a far greater extent than other children from the anxiety it feels in regard to the brother or sister whom it is forever expecting. It also suffers from feelings of guilt because of unconscious aggression against them in their imaginary existence inside the mother's body. The only child has no opportunity to develop a positive relation to a real brother or sister in reality, which often makes it more difficult for the only child to adapt itself to society, Mrs. Klein believed.

At other times, Erna appeared to identify the imaginary brother and sister with her mother and father. Then, she hated the imaginary siblings. Because of the guilt that followed her destructive feelings toward her parents, she would usually have an attack of depression after her wish for a brother or sister. Mrs. Klein said that these fantasies were part of the reason it was impossible for Erna to be on good terms with other children. She feared them as enemies because of her own hatred toward her imaginary brothers and sisters.

When Erna was two-and-a-half-years old, and again at three-and-a-half, she shared her parents' bedroom during a summer holiday. The psychic effects of watching them during sexual intercourse became evident in her analysis, Mrs. Klein said. It was after the first summer that Erna's neurosis came out in full force, when she started sucking her thumb and masturbating all the time.

The sight of her parents in bed "enormously intensified her

sense of frustration and envy in regard to her parents and had raised to an extreme pitch her sadistic phantasies and impulses against the sexual gratification they were obtaining," Mrs. Klein stated.

There was a period in Erna's analysis during which, in her games, she depicted her parents in sexual intercourse in various ways. Afterward she would explode in a fury of frustration. She also had an imaginary child who shared its parents' bedroom and had to look at what went on in their bed. If it interrupted them in any way, it was beaten. Erna, playing the mother, would put the child to bed to get rid of it so that she could return to her husband's side in bed.

Erna was toilet-trained at the age of one, and her conflicting feelings about this early restriction of her pleasure came out during her analysis. At times she treated her feces as poisonous; at other times she pretended to bake and eat them or hand them to Mrs. Klein.

There had been "outward success" in training her but "a completely internal failure," according to Mrs. Klein. At one time Erna played the part of a severe governess who ill treated a child who had dirtied itself. In this scene, Erna was showing how she felt in her early childhood when her toilet training had begun and she believed she was losing the excessive love she had enjoyed as a baby. Another time Erna played at being a child that had dirtied itself. Mrs. Klein, as the mother, was ordered to scold the child, whereupon the child dirtied herself even more out of defiance. Then she vomited up "bad food" her mother had fed her.

Erna came to Mrs. Klein's office for 575 hours of treatment over a period of two-and-a-half years. The analysis was broken off "for external reasons." (Mrs. Klein did not state what these were—the family might have moved away, or lacked money to continue, or thought Erna had improved enough.) Mrs. Klein did not consider the analysis by any means complete, even though Erna had improved in many ways.

For one, her compulsive masturbation, conducted in front of Mrs. Klein and everyone else, had ceased. For another, Mrs. Klein's office, which at first had looked "like a battlefield" after Erna had been there, now remained orderly as the sessions progressed. At the start Mrs. Klein had told Erna that she must not attack her physically but that she could get angry at toys or other objects in the room. Erna would "break her toys or cut them up, knock down the little chairs, fling the cushions about, stamp her feet on the sofa, upset water, smudge paper, dirty the toys or the washing basin, break out into abuse, and so on . . . ."

As Mrs. Klein helped Erna to understand the causes of her rage, the little girl's anger subsided. She became content with hurriedly throwing down cushions before she left, giving up her former destructive acts. Toward the end of her analysis, she left the room calmly. She did not even indulge in the outbreak of rage she always showed when Mrs. Klein told her the hour was at an end.

Erna's relationship to her mother and father vastly improved. She became easier to live with. She now experienced genuine feelings of love for her father—since she was not so completely dominated by hate and fear, the direct Oedipal relationship could begin to establish itself, Mrs. Klein pointed out. At the same time, her fixation on her mother lessened. The sadism diminished in her fantasies, which became fewer in number and less intense. As her unconscious hatred of her mother grew more conscious, she began to criticize her with frankness, as a real person. At the same time, she showed motherly and tender feelings toward her older toy-child.

Erna now slept normally and was no longer depressed. She looked more childlike, as was proper to her age, Mrs. Klein noted. She was also able to learn her lessons more quickly.

Erna was a little girl who had tried by every means to maintain a dream world and escape reality, according to Mrs. Klein. One cause of her retreat was her excessive fear of her parents, especially her mother. It was in order to lessen this fear "that Erna was driven to imagine herself as a powerful and harsh mistress over her mother, and this led to a great intensification of her sadism," Mrs. Klein added.

As this little girl learned to express her feelings and know what she felt, she no longer had to be so angry. She could give up much of the exaggerated fantasy life that had been draining her of the strength to cope with reality.

# The Abandoned Doll

Among the types of cases once considered hopeless, but now treated by psychoanalysts, are those that fall on the borderline between neuroses and psychoses.

The "borderline" patient as a rule is afraid to embark on any human relationship. As a result, he leads an empty, isolated, emotionally impoverished life, devoid of loved ones, friends, even acquaintances. He is difficult to help in analysis because he has never learned to tolerate frustration and his judgment of reality is poor.

This makes the development of what is called "a working alliance" between him and the analyst, a problem of central importance, since the success of an analysis depends on the existence of this working alliance.

Dr. Walter A. Stewart has treated a number of such patients. Generally, he says, these patients have experienced "markedly" traumatic periods early in their childhood. Often their mothers are described as selfish, possessive, seductive, inconsistent, domineering, and acting as rivals to their children. These mothers treat a child as an extension of themselves and prevent it from developing its own identity.

An abstract of this case appeared in *The Psychoanalytic Quarterly,* Vol. XXX, No. 1 (January 1961). The details are published here for the first time. The case illustrates the establishment of a satisfactory working alliance which then made possible the recovery of important memories from the patient's first year of life.

¶A twenty-nine-year-old woman started analysis with Dr. Stewart, following one year with another analyst. She had refused to listen to anything the first analyst said, or to talk about herself.

When Dr. Stewart first saw her, he noted that she looked about twenty years old. She was short, dark-haired, and rather broad-shouldered. "She walked with her legs held stiffly, which gave her a rolling gait, reminiscent of a walking doll," went his description. "She spoke in a slow, dispassionate manner."

She reported details of her current life in an offhand and self-deprecatory manner. Of the previous year's treatment, she said she was lucky to get out alive—literally meaning that she had been afraid the analyst would kill her.

Her major complaint was a feeling of isolation. She expressed a wish for warmer, closer contact with people, but next added that she found human relationships too burdensome and preferred to remain uninvolved. Showing little concern about it, she mentioned that she was a heavy drinker and actively homosexual. At this point, she spoke of being afraid to be left alone in a room with a doll and said this fear had existed since early childhood.

Her life consisted of working as a secretary during the day and watching animated cartoons on television at night. Weekends she spent drinking in various homosexual bars. She said she had gone into analysis in order to turn into a man, and since now she realized this was impossible, she wondered if she needed further treatment.

In spite of her isolated, pseudo-tough attitude, Dr. Stewart sensed in her a desperate need for someone with whom she could feel safe.

In the early phase of the analysis, she treated herself as a robot or doll-like figure with no feelings. When she recounted her dreams, she never spoke of any emotions in them, and expressed surprise when Dr. Stewart said that her feelings might be relevant.

She wanted to think of the analyst as an impersonal scientist who looked upon her as an experimental guinea pig. She could not tolerate his silence, yet she was afraid of his speaking. She did not feel she could be curious about him, for when he commented once that she seemed to have some curiosity about him, she responded, "Do you want me to get killed? In bringing this up, you are trying to torture me."

Another time when she had to cancel some sessions, she felt this amount of self-assertion would end in the analyst's death. She tried to dispose of this fear by claiming he was an automaton without feelings. Then she remarked that this attitude made her seem too much like her mother. She said, "I don't like putting you aside, like putting you in the corner and saying to you, 'I'll tell *you* when you can move.' " She ended this session by turning this attitude back onto herself, becoming the automaton doll, silent, distant, or, as she phrased it, "out in left field."

In spite of her attitude, however, she told Dr. Stewart of certain details in her early life. To him, it became apparent that her mother was a seductive and narcissistic woman who sulked when she was not the center of attention. During the patient's childhood, the mother would frequently threaten to leave home and go to live on a desert island. During the patient's years of puberty, when her father was away on business much of the time, the mother insisted on the girl sharing her double bed and would embrace her from behind.

The mother's intrusiveness and rivalry with her daughter became apparent in her curiosity about the patient's analysis, Dr. Stewart noted. She wanted her daughter to describe her sexual feelings, but wound up telling her daughter intimate details of her own sexual life. She also told her daughter of a dream in which she, the mother, seduced the man for whom her daughter worked.

In contrast to the undesirable intimacy which existed between the patient and her mother, the patient had never had much contact with her father and most communication with him went through her mother who would then repeat his responses to the patient. She had two brothers, both tall and blonde, in contrast to her shortness and dark hair.

She recalled that, at the age of two, she was a very pretty little child in a "doll-like way," and that her parents actually called her a little French doll.

Between the ages of three and six, she suffered a number of traumatic experiences, according to Dr. Stewart. These included the birth of her two younger brothers, a tonsillectomy following a series of colds, and a seduction by a fourteen-year-old uncle. Shortly after her second brother was born, she had nightmares in which a doll came alive. These nightmares were followed by her doll phobia, which had obsessed her over the years.

When she was a little girl, she wanted to be a priest and this wish persisted until she was eight. She turned into a marked tomboy, with fantasies of becoming a ruthless gangster. This showed the strength of her masculine wishes and her poor awareness of reality, Dr. Stewart stated.

While the outstanding characteristic of her mother was a prurient preoccupation with sexual matters, her father was preoccupied with dirt and bad odors. The young woman said that if her father looked at a beautiful view, somewhere he would find a dump. When he was a child, his family had lived as squatters in deserted shacks in the New Jersey flats. He had two sisters, both of whom were alcoholic and promiscuous. He repeatedly told his daughter that the trouble with women was they "overdid" everything.

The father's difficult early life at first seemed to explain why, even at twenty-nine, his daughter was treated as an irresponsible child and her own wishes almost completely ignored, according to Dr. Stewart. She was forced to go to church in spite of her deep aversion—both parents manipulated her under the guise of "doing her good." They did nothing for pleasure; they played golf because it was good exercise, and each one justified the other's drinking by saying it was good for him or her to relax. These therapeutic relaxations were not considered necessary for the daughter, though, Dr. Stewart observed.

One time during her analysis they became impatient with her drinking, which was regular and methodical but not particularly excessive. They hid the bottles in a closet in her own room and told her they would have her locked up in an insane asylum if she drank again. In spite of this concern about her morals, they ignored the obvious symptoms of her illness.

Shortly after, her father again criticized her for drinking. She lost control of herself and started to kick and hit him. She fell on some broken glass, severely lacerating her leg. To quiet her, her father was forced to sit on her.

The violence of this outbreak frightened her and her parents (and her analyst as well, commented Dr. Stewart). Her father phoned Dr. Stewart the next day, after receiving permission from his daughter to call, and told Dr. Stewart that he felt he could not keep his daughter in the house any longer. He had persuaded his own doctor that she should be committed to a mental hospital.

Dr. Stewart suggested that she be permitted to move away from home and assured the father that she was capable of caring for herself. The father agreed quickly to this suggestion. Then he told Dr. Stewart that he felt the analyst should know that the patient was an adopted child. She had been adopted, he explained, because his wife had not been able to conceive. It was not until two years after the adoption that she had her first child.

Dr. Stewart noted that the explanation seemed unlikely since the adoption occurred only a little more than a year after the marriage of her supposed parents. It seemed improbable they would adopt a child after so short a period of time. Therefore, he gently asked the father if his daughter were not really the illegitimate child of one of his sisters. The father hesitatingly admitted that this was true.

Dr. Stewart said that, in retrospect, this should have been clear from the patient's dreams and associations. Although he had many times interpreted her fear of being like her aunts (one of whom was actually her mother), he had only preconsciously been aware of the actual relationship, he said. He added, "It seems equally clear that the patient had a close to conscious suspicion of the truth. Many of the 'parents' fears about the patient's behavior and the sense of being evil could now be better understood."

In spite of the fact that it was a Sunday, Dr. Stewart called the patient immediately and arranged to see her. He saw her twice that day. He informed her of the newly discovered fact and they discussed her reaction to it. She was both upset and relieved. She felt now, for the first time, she could understand aspects of her life and the attitudes of her adopting parents more clearly. She also was moved by the fact that they had cared enough for her to want to adopt her.

It emerged that the patient had been frequently and seriously ill in the first eighteen months of her life. Her real mother was incapable of caring for her and she had been left in a "home" for many months. The serious illnesses had also required repeated hospitalizations. On the last occasion she nearly died and it was clear that unless she received better care her chances for survival were poor. It was for this reason her aunt and uncle, whom she called mother and father, adopted her.

During the first few years of her analysis, the young woman was afraid of developing any emotional tie to Dr. Stewart. She became puzzled by the feelings she did develop, confused both by their strength and their transience. After a few hours of relatively good emotional contact with him, she would suddenly feel empty and distant—as if he and she were on "two slabs of ice in the Arctic, caught in a current, and that we would drift apart, out of sight."

As an attachment slowly developed, she spoke of fears of merging, losing her identity, and bizarre periods of fugue-like states in which she felt enclosed in a fog or possessed by an evil spirit. At home she would sit in her chair unable to move for half an hour; on one occasion she smashed her hand against the wall until it was hideously bruised, and on another, had to hold her right hand with her left to restrain herself from striking out.

She tended to turn every interpretation into a confirmation of her evil, destructive self. For example, at one session she mentioned her sexual feelings for the analyst. This was followed by the thought of leaving her parents' home and renting a room in the city. (This was before her fight with her father.) The juxtaposition of these two thoughts were interpreted by Dr. Stewart as representing her fear of having sexual feelings while her mother was around, and her belief that if she were living in the city she would feel safe from her mother and free to have sexual feelings. The following session, she announced that now she could see that the only reason she wanted to rent a room was in order to masturbate. In another session she told Dr. Stewart, "I hate to think you suspect me of putting fish hooks in everything. It is like my mother. It is as if I had some diseased thing inside me. Like the time I left the closet door open and Dad bumped his head on it. Mother said, 'You nearly knocked your father out.' I don't think now that I left it open for that purpose. Also you know he moves pretty fast and he doesn't watch where he is going. I think that played a part too."

It became clear that any interpretation directed toward the patient's understanding of her aggressive or sexual feelings had only the meaning that she was bad. The interpretation seemed to confirm her worst life-long fears. It appeared that the first analysis had stalemated on this issue. Dr. Stewart, to avoid this outcome, accompanied each interpretation involving her drives with an added comment that showed her the way in which the impulses could be tamed and used in useful ways. By weaving together the drives and the patient's more sublimated goals, he reduced her fear of her impulses and created an identity. She described it as taming a savage who lived inside of her.

By this method of interpretation, he said, a workable therapeutic alliance slowly developed, one in which the patient became increasingly able to look at her own behavior and voice her feelings in the analytic setting. Along with these first transference feelings, she began to bathe carefully each evening because she was afraid the analyst would appear in her dreams. By this time she had come to understand her fear of men, and her longing for closeness to her mother, and had been able to give up her homosexuality.

But the central problem of her illness still remained. This was her fear of people, which found expression in the symptom of the doll phobia. The doll was at various times equated with herself, her older brother, his and her father's penis, her mother, her mother's breast, and her dead grandfather.

This central issue became clearer in connection with the start of a summer vacation and separation from the analyst. She expressed indirectly her expectation of missing him for the first time. Even this degree of "contact" was too much for her and she could only conceive of it in terms of total domination or total submission. She felt, therefore, that it would be unfair and even dangerous to let him know she might be thinking about him during the summer. If he did not know it, it would be all right; it would not alter his behavior or "imprison" him. She, in turn, would not want him to think about her, since this would mean she was "possessed" or "captured." Dr. Stewart interpreted her fear of using him as a lifeless object and of his using her in a similar manner. She related these feelings to her doll phobia. The doll, he noted, represented to her a person "who had come under this Svengali type of domination."

"The patient felt that inside a doll there is a spirit that wants to be free, self-directive, and not subject to someone else's direction," he said. He mentioned to her the interest she showed in the Pygmalion story. She corrected him, saying the image was more like Aladdin and the lamp, when the genie was liberated from the lamp but could be returned to his imprisonment at Aladdin's wish, and even when liberated, was still a slave forced to do Aladdin's bidding.

This brought to her mind an experience of feeling "possessed" while watching a television show in which one woman was possessed by the soul of a murdered woman. The patient also recalled wondering what happened to her image in the mirror when she stood to one side—was it still there, or conversely, was she herself now invisible? She mentioned her fear of being merged with her mother, and a recent "wake" she had attended where she half expected the dead woman suddenly to move. She said that she felt that if she ever expressed any positive feelings for someone, she would be "shoved aside and forgotten," or, conversely, that she might be enslaved and endlessly preyed upon.

The pursuit of these feelings led to the final and most dramatic phase of the analysis, Dr. Stewart said, in which repressed memories from her first year of life emerged. They revolved around the time in which she was in the "home."

She started off by saying that she felt part of her family in a way she never had before. There came to mind the smell of tweed, which reminded her of her dead grandfather whom she remembered with great tenderness. Almost in a trance, she recalled the feeling of being in diapers and feeling "disgusting." Then, breathing rapidly and speaking in a halting way, she said, "Oh, that bitch, she was dressed in white and blue." Then she spoke of seeing a small-boned, olive-complexioned woman. It turned out that this woman was the worker on the ward who took care of her in the "home." The patient remembered her as noisy and grim. When she made up the crib, she would leave the toys, which the patient's mother had brought her, out of her reach.

The next series of memories she described as "oozing out of her like perspiration." She recalled a visit from her mother and an argument between her mother and the head of the "home" about the baby being neglected. She remembered they pried her hands open to force her to let go of her mother. After her mother left she was terrified of the nurses. She said, in recalling the scene, "It was so awful, there aren't words."

The next memory was introduced by a dream in which she was telling the analyst of a party and he asked what was being celebrated. At this, she awoke with great anxiety, aware that the phrases, "Tell me a story," and "Happy Birthday" were going through her mind. During the session that day, she recalled that her mother gave her a book, *The Story of the Three Bears*. "What struck me was that they all lived together," she said.

During the next week she recalled bit by bit another, more traumatic experience. She began one hour by lying on the couch in a very tense manner; she had a marked "startle" response and said she was listening for a noise. Next, what came to her mind was a memory of a dead baby with its arms raised in the air, its back arched, and its eyes opened. She identified this baby as one who had been in the crib next to hers while she was in the "home." She recalled the baby was a blue-eyed girl who could walk around in her crib. The patient had been vastly amused by the older baby's antics. As she spoke of this, her throat hurt, and it was clear she was on the edge of screaming and crying.

She continued to remember more details. One night this blue-eyed child had been tied to her crib. A broad white band had been placed across her chest to hold her down. The patient recalled the little baby had screamed and cried most of the night and then had suddenly stopped crying. The patient was glad the noise had ceased, but she also felt frightened. Then, with a rising sense of horror, the patient said, "When dawn came, I could see her, just her outline. As it got lighter I realized—she must have suffocated."

The dead baby's arms were raised in the air, she said, because it had tried to push out from under the band which held it down.

As a baby in the home, the patient must have had the tragic experience of seeing another little baby die in the crib next to her. This memory and others, concerning rats that infested the home, could be dated to a time when the patient was between fourteen and eighteen months old, Dr. Stewart said.

As she recalled the traumatic experiences of her very early life and lived through them once again, she became less frightened, more self-assertive, and for the first time was able to feel fond of and even to hug the aunt who had adopted her. "For the first time she felt like a daughter, and not like an unwelcome, parasitic, contaminated, devouring rat," commented Dr. Stewart. "She no longer had the need for the defensive doll-like self-de-animation."

In his summary of the case, Dr. Stewart pointed out that, by feeling like a doll, the patient believed she could not be hurt nor would she be able to hurt others for dolls are incapable of any feeling or action: the doll-like attitude allowed her to control her untamable destructive clinging and eating.

Her early marked maternal deprivation, followed by her adoption, the births of her "brothers," really her cousins, and the feeling of being unacceptable to her adoptive mother and father, had made her emotional investment in her aunt, whom she called "mother," "minimal," according to Dr. Stewart. He described the problem as "a relationship with the 'unsatisfying object,' " quoting Dr. Willi Hoffer who wrote, "Perhaps we should regard the interplay between self and object as the central paradox of emotional development: that the child needs his mother's love in order to be able to love himself, in order to be able to do without her love; then he should be able to love another person as he was loved by his mother."

Dr. Stewart declared that this process of development had been damaged in the patient. She could neither love nor trust herself or others. She had a deep, life-long enmity toward both any person to whom she might become attached and her own instinctual needs. She sensed that if her defense of stoical indifference broke down, she would be overwhelmed by her needs, which she expected once again would be frustrated in the analytic setting.

In treating this borderline patient, Dr. Stewart pointed out that both the stalemate of indifference and "the catastrophic consequences of premature interpretations" can be avoided by special and early attention to the particular fears of the patient. He recommended that the analyst accept the "reality" of the frustrations experienced by the patient at the hands of his parents and admit their unavoidable repetition in the analytic setting.

"The analyst should acknowledge that analysis, like war, is sometimes hell," he put it.

This acceptance by the analyst promotes the patient's trust in him, a trust which is prerequisite to any analytic success. In the neurotic patient, this trust develops silently, Dr. Stewart said, whereas in the borderline patient it must be cultivated and takes time. But only as the patient can accept the analytic "contract," can the therapeutic alliance develop and analytic work progress.

This acceptance also leads to the analyst's becoming a person whose love and respect the patient needs. And only in this way will anger at frustration become tamed and capable of mastery. "Trust and the need for love make possible the toleration of frustration,"

Dr. Stewart declared. "They make the child educable and the patient analyzable."

It was a great step forward for this young woman when, in the face of frustration, instead of feeling isolated and "out in left field," she became depressed. It was then that her need for the love of the analyst triumphed over her "angry repudiation" of him.

At the end of her treatment, which lasted for eight years, the patient held an important executive position. She had completely given up homosexuality and had fallen in love with a man. She took part in an active social life and held her drinking within social limits.

Dr. Stewart, who has kept up with her continuing progress, describes her now as a self-respecting person, outgoing and friendly, no longer needing to repress feelings by identifying with a doll.

# A Wheeze Instead of a Sock

Psychoanalysts have been very successful in easing physical ailments caused by emotional problems, known as psychosomatic illnesses. The physical pains—headaches, sinus, constant colds, ulcers, colitis, among others—are often among the earliest symptoms to disappear when treatment begins.

The relationship between emotional conflicts and asthma was made clear in the book *One Little Boy* by the late Dorothy Baruch (published by Julian Press, Inc., in 1952). Dr. Baruch, who wrote the book with "the medical collaboration" of Dr. Hyman Miller, her husband, was a child psychologist and author of *New Ways in Discipline, Parents Can Be People,* and *Glass Houses of Prejudice.*

Her study showed how the asthma attacks that a seven-year-old boy had suffered since the age of three disappeared after psychotherapy. The little boy, Kenneth, also had been failing in school, and as a result of the help he received he became one of the top pupils in his class.

The book also reported the treatment of a family, since his parents went into group therapy. This enabled them to look at their own problems more realistically and indirectly helped their young son.

Dr. Baruch graphically described the way in which the emotional conflicts of a mother and father may affect a child, for children react with great sensitivity to everything in the atmosphere, the unspoken as well as the spoken. As the author put it, "Feelings and thoughts are not absent because they are not spoken. *Not-heard* does not mean *not-present* . . . a child may sense his parents' unconscious feelings . . . ."

She also emphasized that every child takes both little and big events from the world about him and weaves fantasies around them that may be strange and primitive. He may also misinterpret his parents' feelings and actions. He may imagine he is more wronged, more threatened, less loved than he actually is. The resentment, anxiety, fear, and guilt which color his fantasies then loom out of all proportion and his emotions hold great terror for him.

The same basic thoughts and feelings in one child may cause conflicts that result in asthma or failure in school, while in a second child, they may result in problems of discipline, problems with other children, or personality problems. In a third child, they may cause no problems, because he has been given more love and understanding than the others. All people have to cope with the same instinctual drives and needs. If as children they feel wanted and loved, they learn how to handle them. But those who do not feel wanted or loved may face a life-long struggle with their deeper emotions.

¶Kenneth was a big boy for his age, seven years and eight months. Although sturdy in form and build, he did not give the feeling of sturdiness: his shoulders drooped; his eyes, widely set and intelligent, seemed to perceive but hide what they saw; he had pale freckles on his sensitive face; and fair hair.

His young mother, Cathy, visited Dr. Baruch to ask her to take Kenneth as a patient, because he was failing in school and the principal had said he would have to repeat the second grade. As she spoke of Kenneth, his mother's hands trembled when she lit a cigarette. She had dark eyes, dark hair, and little expression on her face except for an occasional, polite smile.

She described Kenneth as "a perfectly normal boy" who didn't have any particular problems. She said he was very bright and she could not understand his failing in school. His father, a young engineer, had been at the head of his class in college. Cathy had never gone to college, had regretted it, and confessed she might have pushed Kenneth too hard to get good marks. As Cathy spoke, Dr. Baruch sensed in her a deep suffering, although she appeared outwardly controlled.

Kenneth had been "a good baby," "clean," "a timid child, not pushy," talked before he was a year old, never quarreled with his brother, Brad, three years younger, or the other boys in the neighborhood. He had no friends and did not seem interested in other boys, his mother said.

His asthma had started when she was pregnant with her second son. She said of it, "It's terrible to see a child almost strangling, gasping for breath almost every night."

Dr. Baruch agreed to accept the little boy for therapy. At the first session she told Kenneth that if she knew how he felt about things she probably would be able to help him. She assured him that the most important thing to her was what *he* wanted to do. She asked him what he thought about that.

He replied in a flat tone, almost a whisper, "It doesn't matter." Dr. Baruch noticed that he breathed with difficulty. She felt he was "a hurt child, that something or many things had hurt him so much that he dared not speak of his wishes."

Dr. Baruch conducted play therapy with Kenneth. She asked him to paint and play with clay and puppets and other toys. At first he said he would "rather not play with anything." He merely stood in the playroom in front of the toy closet, wheezing with asthma.

Dr. Baruch had told him he could call her "Dorothy." He looked at her piteously and said, "Please, Dorothy, I don't want to do anything . . . Please don't make me." She assured him she would not, that he could do what he wished. He then climbed into her lap and curled up like a helpless puppy, wanting only to be held. He lay there quietly until the session ended. Dr. Baruch noted that as he went out the door, he breathed more quietly.

One fact stood out, the author said. Kenneth was so hungry for love that he wanted to slip back to the start of his life to make up for what he felt he had lacked. He wanted a second chance at being a baby so he might gather into himself the feeling of being loved for himself, not for what he accomplished.

During the next few sessions all he did was climb onto Dr. Baruch's lap and stay there. He wanted contact, as though she were his mother. He experimented further by whining softly like a baby, then sucking his thumb.

After a few such sessions, he did not seek her lap any more but started to play with the clay and paints and toys. He chose a box of soldiers armed with bayonets, machine guns, and cannons. He placed them behind hillocks in two opposing armies, the Americans and the "enemies." He slaughtered the "enemies." Then he made miniature bombs out of clay. He took puppets and named them "the father," "the mother," "the boy," and "the brother," and let the bombs fall on all of them, killing them. He pretended to kill "Dorothy" herself.

As he expressed his anger in play, Kenneth's asthma disappeared. His anger "was draining out through the drama of killing, it did not need for the moment to drain out in asthma," said Dr. Baruch. Kenneth's sickness and failure in school had been "camouflages," she explained, through which he was saying, "I'm being good, not naughty. I can't help it, after all, if I fail or am sick." At the same time, he was turning back on himself the feelings that he was deserted and destroyed, punishing himself with illness and failure.

Dr. Baruch believed that if Kenneth could reach the point where he did not have to deny his aggressive feelings, the energy he used for hiding them would then be freed for work and play, for friendship and love.

Dr. Baruch, meanwhile, encouraged Kenneth to express anger in his play and to ask whatever questions he wanted. Kenneth, like all children, was very curious about how babies are born and how mothers and fathers create them. Dr. Baruch realistically and gently answered all his questions. He also showed a great curiosity about his own body. He told how his grandmother, when he visited her, told him not to touch his penis and made him feel he was "bad" if he did so.

There is no child alive who, at times, is not angry at his parents, Dr. Baruch pointed out, for hate exists side by side with love. A child needs love and understanding in order to be able to accept, then control, his anger. His basic hungers need to be nourished so his anger will not be too great. If they are not, he will grow more demanding and cunning and, in one way or another, cling to immaturity as though it were his only salvation.

In a home where a child is allowed to show no anger, he will control it, as Kenneth did, but his fantasies of revenge will become intense. He must then overly control and punish himself. He relegates his fantasies to his unconscious and uses his energy to keep them buried there.

Cathy visited Dr. Baruch from time to time and at one session lost her reserve. She put her hands over her face, dug her nails into her cheeks, and wailed, "Oh, I know it. I know it. It's all my fault. I'm no good for Kenneth. I should never have had any children . . . I know I'm ruining them. I didn't really want them." Neither did her husband, she said, but she had persuaded him after her mother had persuaded her. She told Dr. Baruch further that she thought she was "too self-centered," and her sons felt she pushed them aside.

At times, she admitted, she locked Kenneth in his room because she was afraid she could not control her feelings and might hurt him as she had once tried to hurt her small brother when they were children. In a rage she had thrown him to the floor and banged his head against the floorboards, wanting to kill him. Then she stopped herself, stood up, pushed him into another room, and locked the door to protect him from her fury.

She said that Kenneth, besides suffering his first asthma attacks when she was pregnant with Brad, had also reverted at that time to wetting his bed (as children often do when they know a rival is on the way or appears). She commented that Kenneth's regressive behavior had disgusted her.

Dr. Baruch theorized that the mother had been unable to nourish her son's "love-hunger" because of her own "love-hunger" as a child. Kenneth felt deprived of love and became exceedingly hostile, but blocked out his feelings. His doctor mentioned the fact to Dr. Baruch that when Kenneth came to him for injections for his asthma, which were painful ones, the boy would never show any emotion.

It became apparent that Kenneth not only felt rejected when, as a hungry baby, he had been afraid his mother would not feed him (which meant, to him, that she wanted to starve him to death) but he also felt his mother's rejection of him as a male, Dr. Baruch stated. He lived in constant fear of being hurt. He often made a clay figure which was obviously himself and said of the figure: "He's an unhappy boy. Poor thing! He wants to be happy. He keeps wondering how. He's a cockeyed kid. See him? See him; how ugly? Mothers don't like ugly boys." Then he went into what was a recurrent theme: "Booms! There he trips. His head is almost off. His arms are almost off. His legs are almost off and one of them got much too short."

Then came a fantasy that was a replica of what he was doing in reality. "Poor boy! He has to go to bed now and stay there and his mother *has* to feed him at least once every day. He's happy at last. His worries are gone."

Dr. Baruch pointed out that, by being sick, Kenneth could make sure of receiving attention from his mother as he coughed and wheezed, while at the same time indirectly venting hostility against her. He was unable to express resentment openly, finding it hard even to fight with his brother, of whom he was extremely jealous. He told Dr. Baruch after they were fairly well along in treatment, "Sometimes I want to let go. Over some little nothing, almost. Some little thing happens; only it isn't little when it gets to me. It seems big. I guess because it sets off something *big* inside me. The biggest wish to SOCK that you ever knew. It's so big that if I socked anybody with that much steam I—I—think I'd explode."

Very simply, said Dr. Baruch, Kenneth had described what

many people never come to understand—that he was so afraid he might act on his inner anger that he had kept himself tightly in check, almost immobilized. He punished himself for what he thought were bad wishes by feeling guilty, falling ill, and failing in school. It was as though he were saying to himself he must not be aware of his feelings or they would burst and destroy him and his world. A child will accept the necessary denials and frustrations of life without too much anger if his emotional needs are satisfied by his mother in the helpless beginnings of his life when he cannot fend for himself, Dr. Baruch said. But Kenneth had never felt such security.

His parents decided to go into group therapy, and although it looked at one point as if their marriage might break up (each was attracted temporarily to another person), they decided to stay together, realizing they would have the same problems within themselves no matter with whom they lived. They faced their sexual incompatibility and tried to understand the reasons for it. They realized how Kenneth had responded to their moods and quarreling with his own unhappiness.

Kenneth saw Dr. Baruch regularly for two-and-a-half years, then occasionally for the next three whenever he felt he wanted to. Dr. Baruch believed he could at last manage his feelings of anger without denying them. He had, she said, acquired the basis for "true *self-control*—for managing the outflow of feelings, neither denying them nor letting them run wild." He saw what he could do and what he could not do in more realistic terms.

He had realized, too, that he could feel certain pleasurable sensations in his body without believing he was "dirty" or "bad." He knew he had to control his sexual feelings not by blocking or denying or paralyzing them, but by finding acceptable ways to express them in accordance with his age.

In spite of the problems that his mother and father had not yet worked out, Kenneth was doing well, Dr. Baruch felt. His asthma was gone. He told Dr. Baruch it was "a good feeling" to know he could come to see her whenever he needed her but that he was "real busy at school now and real busy playing." He added, "When I first started with you I didn't need time for playing. I didn't have one true friend then. Now I have lots. I think now I need more time for myself and my friends."

In discussing the case of Kenneth, Dr. Baruch concluded that "the realest part" of the picture of childhood comes from what a child sees and hears and feels around him, and even more, from what he makes of this in his mind. He gets cues, either openly or subtly, from what his parents mean to each other. He ties these in with the sensations of his own body.

She said, "His impressions spread their wings in fantasy and mate in flight with wishes that he often feels should-not-be and with guilt and anxiety. And these in turn let misshapen offspring wing their way into adulthood to destroy the richness of mating and loving and creation and birth."

# The Rabbit Larger Than
the Hunter

The aging person not only can be helped by a psychoanalyst but the study of his mental processes can contribute to research in psychoanalysis.

The following case shows that no matter how young or old a person may be, the unconscious part of the mind is never altered. As the author of the case, Dr. Martin Grotjahn, points out, "An interesting fact in the psychology of old age is that as a rule in a man the fear of castration with all its power and violence does not diminish . . . because the id does not participate in this process of growing older."

The "id" is that part of the psyche which is the source of instinctive energy, the reservoir of sexual and aggressive drives. It is dominated by the pleasure principle and impulsive wishing. Its impulses are controlled and censored by our ego and superego.

When Dr. Grotjahn originally wrote the case it was titled "Psychoanalytic Investigation of a Seventy-One-Year-Old Man with Senile Dementia." [It appeared in *The Psychoanalytic Quarterly,* Vol. IX, No. 1 (January 1940).] In the article, Dr. Grotjahn thanked Dr. Karl Menninger for the opportunity to study the case at the Menninger Clinic.

It represents the first detailed psychoanalytic report ever made of an aged person, one who was quite emotionally disturbed. The psychoanalytic investigation was undertaken mainly as a research problem, according to Dr. Grotjahn, "in an attempt to establish and to understand psychological facts such as the development of the psychosis, and to show that such a development is governed by psychological laws." The man's dementia was partially due to cerebral arteriosclerosis.

The study also had the additional purpose of gaining some insight into the reaction of the unconscious toward the process of growing old. According to Dr. Grotjahn, the process of investigation, the nature of the material obtained, the analytic situation, the management of transference, the psychoanalytic interpretation and construction, and further, the scientific and therapeutic goals of a case study of a psychotic are fundamentally different from what is commonly experienced in an average analytic practice.

"Not only is the senile person's relationship to reality changed by his psychotic withdrawal but the reality situation itself is fundamentally changed by the biological and social dependence and helplessness of an old man," he said. This fact and the sexual impotence of old age make the analytic situation similar to child analysis, he pointed out. In both, the analyst "is not a more or less unreal image but a vivid, active part of reality engaged in the management of the patient's life."

During the five months of daily interviews with this patient, Dr. Grotjahn noted that it was apparent the patient personally benefited from the sessions in a number of ways, as well as contributing to the research project.

¶A very tall, old man entered the clinic voluntarily, saying he wished to obtain a statement to the effect that he was "physically and mentally perfect." His eldest daughter accompanied him.

He was called "Dad" Thomas, a nickname by which he was well known. He had been born on a farm. His father, an extremely poor farmer who lived with his wife and children in a small one-room cabin, had died of the measles when the patient was ten years old. At this point, the patient ran away. He never again saw his mother nor any of his brothers or sisters.

At first he made his living as a cowboy, then a professional hunter. He became interested in photography and rejected a very lucrative job as a professional trapshooter to study photographic processes. In 1902, he originated trick photography. His photographs of rabbits larger than their hunters, and of a team of horses hauling an ear of corn so big that it apparently filled the entire wagon, caused a sensation.

He was a very friendly man and people liked to do business with him. However, he was not gregarious enough to join any organizations; he never went to church or gave to charity.

When he was twenty-one he married a girl of sixteen. She was rather quiet and modest and never interfered with what he wanted. He spent most of his time away from home doing business with farmers. His children seldom saw him; he was not very devoted to his family. After his wife died of diabetes, he turned his children out of the home, arranging for the marriage of his eldest daughter, sixteen at the time, and placing the two younger ones in foster homes.

A few months later, he remarried. None of his children were allowed to enter his home from that time on. His second marriage was an unhappy one, for this wife tried to dominate him and they fought angrily.

At the age of sixty-four, in 1929, "Dad" Thomas, who never had an accident, began to drive his car very carelessly and one day crashed into a telephone pole. He lost consciousness for hours, one leg was broken and he suffered from a severe loss of blood; his condition was considered critical. He recovered but from then on seemed emotionally disturbed.

He got in touch with his eldest daughter, whom he had not seen for nearly fifteen years, and asked her, because she had studied architecture, to plan a house for him and supervise its building. He was then in the advertising business, and, accepting his daughter's suggestion, made his son, whom he also had not seen in years, president of the company and devoted all his time to building the house.

He divorced his second wife in 1935 on grounds of cruelty. The week following the divorce, he announced his intention to marry a housemaid but he did not. Instead he became ardent with every girl he met, proposing marriage to several. He became worried about his sexual potency and consulted many physicians for advice. He believed he could "cure" himself, and also cure others "like Christ did." He suddenly became interested in Christian Science, feeling that as a Christian Scientist he had "cured" himself and that he was immune to all illness. He also had the theory he could prevent dust storms, by planting sweet clover, and began to pay large sums of money for selected arid tracts.

In the meantime, his house had been completed and he moved into it after hiring servants. His daughter visited him daily, for he was frightened of being left alone, fearing he would be kidnapped. He threatened to shoot any stranger who approached the house. When his son took his guns away from him, he tried to oust his son as president of the company. He fired all the servants because he thought they were plotting to starve and freeze him to death. He said he believed his friends were being influenced by his children to question his sanity, and therefore was willing to consult a psychiatrist and to enter the Menninger Clinic for observation and examination.

During the first three weeks, Dr. Grotjahn interviewed Mr. Thomas every day for two hours and sometimes longer. The following four months, Dr. Grotjahn saw him regularly every day for an hour. Throughout the day, the patient was under constant observation by nurses who reported daily on his behavior.

He did not lie down on the couch, customary procedure for psychoanalytic patients, because, as Dr. Grotjahn explained, such an act did not seem reasonable to him. Although lying down would not have affected his mode of speaking and acting, it would have made him uncomfortable physically, and, having been a photographer all his life, he liked to look at his physician. Dr. Grotjahn wanted to foster the "transference."

Free association was not even suggested. Mr. Thomas sat in a chair with Dr. Grotjahn at his side where he could see him. Sometimes he looked out of the window at the Kansas countryside. Or he would take a walk with Dr. Grotjahn and talk as they strolled along.

When Dr. Grotjahn first met him, Mr. Thomas asked the

analyst's age, saying, "I am surely twice as old as you." He confessed a sudden and strong confidence in the analyst, saying, "You are the right man to judge whether or not I am crazy."

During the early sessions, he gave a short summary of his life, which agreed with the information furnished by his daughter. He repeated anecdotes which he told everyone in the ward. He was a practical joker, with a tendency to tease and trick his friends in the hospital. He even put sugar in his urine to fool his physician. His stock of stories made him much sought after and well liked among the patients. His great height, slightly demonstrative and old-fashioned manner, and good humor made him an outstanding, singular, and original personality, according to Dr. Grotjahn.

He kept his room and his clothing in filthy condition and objected to having them cleaned. The disorder of his room was increased by his propensity for collecting articles and guarding against them being put in order by others. He had great difficulty finding his belongings, always forgetting where he put letters, cigars, socks and other clothing, and therefore tried to keep everything in sight, either on his desk or dresser. This increased the disorder of his surroundings to the point of complete chaos. His constant fear that he might become hungry and unable to secure food stimulated him to hide in his dresser small quantities of meat, salt, and sugar wrapped in socks or handkerchiefs.

He guarded his false teeth and his golf clubs with special care, living in fear that someone would try to take them from him. He would exhibit two small golf tees saying they were all he could save from the housecleaning.

He was proud of his strength and proud of his appetite. He bragged that he could consume daily an entire bottle of Worcestershire sauce and at every meal six cups of coffee, which he complained were never strong enough. Apparently one purpose in taking in so much fluid was to urinate more often, according to Dr. Grotjahn. He was slightly disoriented—at times Mr. Thomas had difficulty in finding the bathroom although it adjoined his room. Once he was found standing at an open window trying to urinate against a heavy dust storm. He made a joke of this and boasted about it.

His recent and remote memory were deficient. He could not remember the correct dates of important events in his life. He was not even quite sure how old he was. According to some documents he was seventy-one, but to others, seventy-five. During the memory test he volunteered to tell what he knew of past events to prove he had a good memory. The dates he volunteered—Washington's death and some battles of the Civil War—were correct. He could not remember, however, his analyst's name and called him simply "The Dutchman." Whenever he met someone he liked, he referred to him as "another Dutchman." He often remarked, "I do not try to remember names."

He had a simple concept of his mental apparatus. He had, he said, very thick skull bones and consequently his brain was so small that there was room in it for only one idea at a time. This was a satisfactory state because, he explained, there was room only for one *good* idea and no bad ones.

Following his automobile accident, he had lost his sexual potency. When Dr. Grotjahn questioned him about this, in contrast to his usual talkativeness, he answered in monosyllables. He confessed reluctantly that he had trouble with potency even before the accident.

Although the accident was a great psychic and physical trauma he spoke of it with pride to prove that such things "do not get me down." He was "more dead than alive," he said, but he survived. When he left the hospital after a long period of unconsciousness and many blood transfusions, he and his friends believed that if he could live through that experience, he would "never have to die." He did not know how the accident occurred but remembered picking up a boy hitchhiker and, while talking to him, the automobile crashed into a telephone pole.

The patient said that he wanted to be fully potent again so he could marry a third time, this time only "for comradeship." He said he believed that no one his age was potent, but he was by no means sure about this. He told of asking a ninety-three-year-old man when men usually lose their potency, and of being disappointed by the old man's answer: "About that you will have to ask an older man than I am." The patient believed that women, his second wife for example, never lost their sexual desire. He envied his wife and begrudged her this superiority, stating that the only treatment for her "oversexed" condition would be to "shoot her in the trees" or "knock her on the roof."

He denied masturbating, explaining that when he was about twelve he had heard a quack lecture on syphilis and other venereal diseases. The lecture and accompanying wax exhibits had convinced him not to have sexual intercourse before marriage, a decision to which he had held.

He showed strong hypochondriacal fears. He not only asked for reassurance and written statements about his physical condition, but also had to prove by long walks and by his astonishing skill at golf how physically "perfect" he was. He always began the session with the statement that he was physically perfect. His golf technique and his long walks proved he was "the strongest man in this place," he said, and it must therefore follow that he was also mentally perfect.

He repeated with pride a story of visiting people who were sick with measles or whooping cough. At his request they spat in his mouth and even then he did not become infected. Frequently in association with this story he told how his father had died of measles contracted from a child, probably—so it may be assumed, according to Dr. Grotjahn—from the patient himself.

At night he was especially fearful and anxious but was very reluctant to discuss how he felt then except in response to direct questions. He was afraid he would be kidnapped. He closely connected with this fantasy the son who had taken away his shot guns.

His emotional instability became apparent when he began to cry easily, but usually it was equally easy to reassure him, Dr. Grotjahn said. The weeping was often connected with thoughts of his daughter, who he believed had deserted him. Almost every day he wrote her a letter containing the same statement: "If you wish to see your old father alive, come at once." He was somewhat ashamed of his emotional instability, his helplessness, and his dependence upon his daughter.

He enjoyed talking about his invention of trick photography, giving an account of how the ingenious idea came to him. He had been looking at himself through his fingers in a mirror and had thought it would be amusing if he could find a lens that would give a clear picture of the big hand with the small head behind it. He then experimented a long time until he discovered the technique necessary to achieve this idea. The picture with the fingers of his hand larger than his face was his first trick photograph. He carried these thirty-year-old pictures like a talisman in his pocket and was always ready to exhibit them with the stock remark: "It is true; it is a photo. You can see it with your own eyes." He never took pictures of women but he liked to impress women by showing them his pictures.

He slept well as a rule. For the few nights he experienced difficulty in going to sleep, he always gave the same explanation—he had been disturbed by "couples of young people who made love to each other." While maintaining that he never dreamed, he admitted to having once been frightened by a lion's mouth glimpsed in a nightmare.

He treated his analyst like a beloved son, very much in contrast to his mixed feelings about his own son, Dr. Grotjahn noted. Mr. Thomas promised him a position as vice-president of his company and, what meant even more to him, offered some of his hidden food and gave him cigars. He also asked the analyst to sleep in his bed with him in order to verify the nocturnal disturbances and to see for himself the thieves who tried to steal his teeth and his golf clubs.

When he felt depressed, he wanted to die and wished that his heart, "this old mule," be cut out of his chest. Like all his emotions, these periods of depression were neither deep nor of long duration, exhibited mainly during the daily sessions with his analyst, following which Mr. Thomas enjoyed golf and other activities at the hospital. Occasionally the spells of depression culminated in violent outbursts of desperation and tears.

According to Dr. Grotjahn, "an analytic interpretation and construction of a case such as this presents many difficulties and some doubts of its possibility of accomplishment." The material obtained through five months of daily observation was gained more by observing the patient's reaction to reality rather than his free associations (which lead to unconscious wishes). The conclusions drawn from the observations must be more speculative in character than in the average analysis, Dr. Grotjahn pointed out.

The chief obstacle was the lack of knowledge about the patient's early childhood. Few recollections of importance could be recovered, so that the story of his life started rather late.

Dr. Grotjahn stated that a severe castration anxiety appears to have been aroused in Mr. Thomas as a boy when he heard the quack lecture on venereal diseases. Both the lecture and the exhibits not only inhibited masturbation but apparently prohibited sexual relations, which according to his statement, he did not experience prior to marriage.

"The assumption is justified that this castration fear was the reactivation of an incompletely repressed infantile castration threat," the analyst said. "The patient lost his father when he was about ten years old. That, as the patient believed, his father had died of measles, a disease of childhood, provided a possible connection with the patient himself. Fearing the dead father's revenge, he left home never to return. In his later psychotic delusion he himself is immune to measles or any other infection. He reassures himself that the dead father is no threat to him. In the delusion that his first wife might have had syphilis, he gave expression to his direct fear of castration from sexual intercourse."

The patient's later life was dominated by a tremendous castration fear, according to Dr. Grotjahn. Mr. Thomas needed visual restoration of confidence, so he left his mother and family to "see" the world, was proud of his excellent eyesight, using it to become a famous trapshooter. In his castration fear, Dr. Grotjahn said, he chose *visual* pleasure for his profession because with it he fought the typical Oedipus punishment—the loss of eyesight. "The great impression which the lecture on venereal diseases made on him may be partially explained by the fact that this castration shock was brought to him visually. He saw that castration was something that existed in reality. The unconscious function of the patient's trick photography then was to deny castration by showing that all is not what it seems."

The strongest evidence that the invention of trick photography was a way of overcoming his castration anxiety was the manner in which Mr. Thomas got the idea, Dr. Grotjahn believed. He saw his own face (his ego) becoming small and unimportant behind the outstretched, threatening fingers in the mirror. The idea of putting the little face behind the tremendously enlarged fingers was his first concept of trick photography. His pictures soon became known all over the country as millions of copies were sold and laughed at by millions of people. He then conceived the idea of using his photographs for advertising purposes, in effect, inviting everyone to laugh at his castration fear with him.

"The device was always the same—enlarging a minor detail so that it impressed by its disproportionate magnitude. His pictures not only *denied* castration by showing an ear of corn so large that four horses were required to haul it, by showing a rabbit so big it was necessary for the hunter to follow it in an automobile, but they also unmasked the castration fear and *ridiculed* it. For instance, there was the fisherman threatened by a fish as long as the boat, and as the fisherman tried to escape, the fish seized one of his legs and swam away with it."

Dr. Grotjahn pointed out that the coincidence of Mr. Thomas meeting his own unconscious needs with the needs of the populace made his invention a financial success and served further to dispel his castration fear by providing him with money, which among other things, is a symbol of masculine power.

There was still another and perhaps even stronger motive behind the patient's love for photography, Dr. Grotjahn said. Mr. Thomas repeated in his profession in a modern way what Narcissus did when, looking into a pool of water, he saw his own image and fell in love with it. Mr. Thomas made his first trick photograph of himself. His narcissistic pleasure was disguised, for he never pictured himself as youthful and handsome, but rather as a caricature. However, the expression of his face betrayed narcissistic, exhibitionistic pleasure. The photography also may have helped Mr. Thomas meet his sadistic needs, in that he "took" or "shot" pictures revealing people in embarrassing situations or ridiculing them by tricks.

Noting that the patient's illness dated from the time of the automobile accident, Dr. Grotjahn pointed out: "It is not clear whether his ambivalence toward men was an unconscious motivation. Suffice it to say that the accident occurred after picking up a boy, a tramp, and while speaking with this young man, the personification of youthfulness and potency, the patient crashed his car into a telephone pole. The severe loss of blood, the broken bones, and the loss of consciousness brought the patient close to death, the ultimate castration.

"Becoming definitely impotent, he could not relinquish his fight against castration and old age, especially after talking with a much older man who still claimed to be potent and after learning that women apparently do not lose their sexual potency. Trying to prove his potency by pseudosexual activity, he only proved more painfully his impotency . . ."

It became increasingly difficult for the patient to see the realities of his life, his physical and mental defects, his impotency, his age, and his approaching death. According to Dr. Grotjahn, Mr. Thomas "ignored the essentials of things and concentrated on non-essential details." What at first appeared to be a neurotic blind spot, a defense against being aware of his fear of castration, later became the essential feature of his dementia. By making use of his enormous body, he made himself believe he was in perfect physical health and thought this would prove his mental health was perfect as well. Unable to face reality, he preferred to enjoy "life without tomorrow, the life of a child."

His fears of being kidnapped, of losing his money, his teeth and his golf clubs, and his very freedom should he be put in a mental hospital, were a projection of his own hostile, castrating tendencies, Dr. Grotjahn said. He had lived in his cottage with his famous shot guns, beloved symbols of his youth and power, which he attempted to use in self-defense against the "kidnappers." When his son took away the shot guns, it was a terrible blow to the old man, Dr. Grotjahn commented, for he had now lost his last symbol of power—it was a direct father-son castration in reverse and he could not forgive his son, feeling that people would now think there might be something wrong with his mind. His desire for a written statement of his "perfect health" was a desire for protection against his fear and anxiety, and for reassurance and proof that he had not lost his mind, his mental potency.

Dr. Grotjahn pointed out that it was strange that when he got older he turned for love to the children whom he had "so callously abandoned and whom he ignored for the greater part of his life." He became very attached to and dependent on his daughter and made his son his successor as president of the company. Then, when he felt his children thwarted or frustrated him, he turned upon them in rage like "an angry god punishing his children."

The analyst interpreted Mr. Thomas's states of desperation and rage, the very destructive elements of his hostility to his children, and the ease with which he gave up his fortune as signs of a psychotic destructiveness. This narcissistic man had had reason enough to turn his aggressiveness against himself, to hate himself in his weakness, dependence, and impotency. He could not manage adjustment to what he thought was an intolerable reality. "Adjustment to reality," said Dr. Grotjahn, "always includes some expectation for the future . . . But to be old means to be without future so the patient lived in the present without expectation for the future, which could only bring him nearer to castration and death."

The patient showed a childlike dependence upon Dr. Grotjahn. The treatment offered him the pleasure of enjoying a situation new to him, as he depended upon a powerful, helpful, fatherlike person to manage some of his real problems and to offer him protection and reassurance.

Also childlike was the patient's enjoyment of sleep and his bodily functions. A good bowel movement insured for him a fairly happy day. He also apparently got pleasure in filth, and personal uncleanliness and disorder in his room. Urination gave him so much gratification that he urinated as often as possible. He showed real happiness when he was indulging in such forms of oral gratification as talking, joking, and telling dirty stories to his friends.

In summing up, the analyst stated that the psychoanalytic investigation of a single case does not permit generalization and it would be premature to say that it is the "narcissistic person" who reacts to senility with the development of a psychosis.

However, he adds, it is quite clear that growing old is a narcissistic trauma and that someone who has been fairly emotionally mature "may face the effects of aging and death with more calmness than the narcissistic person who, in his imagination, possesses eternal youthfulness."

The strong transference that Mr. Thomas had to the analyst, whom he felt was father and son at the same time, afforded him protection against his castration fear and against his fear of becoming old and insane. Under the guidance of Dr. Grotjahn, he was able to accept some aspects of reality. He agreed to the appointment of a guardian to take care of his fortune, a partial readjustment to reality that he had been unable to make before his admission to the hospital. When he left he felt much more confidence in himself.

# If Love Is Lacking—
# Steal It

Every child, at one time or another, has the impulse to steal or perhaps actually does steal, whether it is a piece of candy from the store, pennies from a mother's purse, or a toy from the child next door. Most people, as they grow up, learn to control this impulse. But some men and women are not able to do so.

As psychoanalysts learned more about the power of unconscious fantasies, the causes of such crimes as theft become clearer. Psychoanalysts began to treat patients who stole and found they could help them understand and check what had been uncontrollable impulses.

The act of stealing, according to Freud, has meaning on many levels. On one level, the thief is stealing the object—the jewel necklace or the mink coat or the $10,000 from the safe. On another level, he is stealing love and attention. On still another level, he seeks punishment. On an even deeper level, he steals what to him was the most valued object in his childhood.

In other words, the stolen object may symbolize a number of things in the mind of the thief, some of which he is unaware. It is easy to understand why he steals the sparkling jewel necklace, the soft mink coat, or the alluring $10,000; it is easy, too, to understand that stealing may represent a demand for love and attention in that the thief is asking for affection and admiration through his daring deed. It is not quite so easy, however, to understand why a thief seeks punishment, or what, to his unconscious, the stolen item represents that is so important he must risk life and limb to get it. In Freudian theory, these two desires are closely tied together. Freud maintained that a thief seeks punishment because of his guilt as a child because of unresolved Oedipal feelings. And the object stolen, Freud believed, unconsciously represents the phallus, the instrument of sexual power that to a child is the most mysterious, dangerous, but cherished object in the world.

If someone has not been able to resolve his early conflicts concerning his mother and father, he may carry his childish wishes and fears into adulthood.

The following case of kleptomania shows how a very intelligent, gifted, young woman was unable to control her impulse to steal. An emotionally deprived childhood had prevented her from giving up her childhood attachment to a father she never really knew but for whom she yearned, and to a dependent, unhappy mother who failed to fill her daughter's psychological needs.

Written by Dr. Sandor Lorand, this case originally appeared as a chapter, "Crime in Fantasy and Dreams and the Neurotic Criminal," in his book *Clinical Studies in Psychoanalysis* (published by International Universities Press in 1950). In it Dr. Lorand discusses a number of the unconscious urges that led to kleptomania on the part of this young woman.

¶A father and his twenty-one-year-old daughter came to the office of Dr. Lorand. The father explained that his daughter was a kleptomaniac. She first began to steal when she was a schoolgirl and had continued on and off ever since.

She was above average in intelligence, had graduated from a conservatory of music, and taught piano. When she visited the homes of her pupils, she would often steal small objects and occasionally even valuable jewelry, which she hid in her room. Sometimes she stole money from her father and stepmother and sent it abroad to an aunt who had brought her up when her mother died.

Dr. Lorand noticed that she found fault with whatever her father said and kept correcting him. After he gave a lengthy description of her acts, Dr. Lorand asked her if his account was true. At first the girl was silent, and then she said that if Dr. Lorand was going to listen to her father's story, she had nothing to say.

"This obviously defiant manner was the keynote of her whole attitude to life," Dr. Lorand noted.

She seemed quite depressed about her uncontrollable stealing, and was willing to try psychoanalytic treatment to rid herself of this compulsion. She visited Dr. Lorand irregularly for years. During that time, he obtained sufficient knowledge about her life to form an opinion of the causes of her kleptomania, as well as to reach some conclusions about kleptomania in general.

She had been born abroad, and was the only child of her parents. Her father emigrated to the United States when she was a baby, never sending for the mother or child. Her mother died when she was twelve, and an aunt took her in, becoming a second mother.

She had no memories, as a little girl, of her father. All she knew of him were occasional letters and money he mailed for her education from the United States. When she was nineteen her father, who had remarried, sent for her. It was then that her real difficulties began.

After she arrived in the United States, her father said she argued incessantly with her stepmother, the one who had urged him to send for his daughter. The father said he did not side with either of them. Then, noticing that money was disappearing from both his wallet and his wife's pocketbook, he started to suspect his daughter. He found some jewelry in her room which he knew she had not brought from Europe and which she could not afford to buy with the money she earned teaching music. When he confronted her with the jewelry, she confessed that she had stolen it from the homes of pupils. It was then her father brought her to see Dr. Lorand.

During her sessions with Dr. Lorand, the girl spoke of her early life. She said she had never known why her mother and father had separated. Her mother, a depressed woman who was constantly crying, told her only that he had gone to America to earn a better living. She asked why her father did not send for them, since he sent money, which seemed to her a sign he was doing well financially, but her mother never answered. So she had to form her own ideas as to why her mother and father had separated. As a little girl, she believed she was not the real child of her parents and that her father could not be her actual father, since her mother insisted on keeping the reasons for his absence a mystery. She felt different from other children she knew, all of whom had fathers.

"Putting ourselves into the place of such a child, we can easily comprehend that the comparison he is bound to make between himself and other children who have homes and families will not dissolve itself easily," Dr. Lorand commented.

Her mother brought her up in an inconsistent fashion, one moment spoiling her and showing intense concern for her welfare; the next moment, sunk in depression, ignoring her completely. After her mother died, her aunt concentrated on her niece's education. Since the girl seemed talented musically, the aunt chose the teaching of piano as her future profession.

As a student, she was considered precocious but stubborn. Since her aunt had no money and her father's contribution seemed to be growing smaller, the girl realized at the age of fourteen that she should contribute something to her board and room. She was able to earn money by helping other children with their music lessons, and thus gained admittance to the homes of wealthy families.

It was at this time, she told Dr. Lorand, that she began to feel life was futile and that the compulsion to steal became very strong. When she got the chance, she stole money which she gave to her aunt. She had sometimes taken books from other children when she lived with her mother, or had stolen candy other children had brought to school. When her mother found out about it, she had punished her daughter. She made the girl return the books.

At the age of seventeen, she became upset because she felt so driven to steal. She gave up going to the homes of children of wealthy parents to avoid the temptation. But even in less well-to-do homes she would find herself taking scarves and other articles of small value, which she hid at home in her dresser. Then, when her father brought her to America at the age of nineteen, she continued stealing.

The girl seemed devoted to her father until her thefts were discovered. Then her antagonism came out into the open. At times she would leave home for days and live with friends, causing her father great distress. She often accused him of abandoning her and her mother and now of forsaking his only sister, who had brought her up. She was convinced that her stepmother had wanted her to live with them only because of her earnings. Her excuse for stealing was that she wanted to send money to her aunt, which was true.

The father admitted to his daughter that he had been at fault each time she made a scene, and she would promise not to steal any more. But her father would subsequently find articles in her possession which he knew she must have taken from someone's home. He would accuse her; she would confess to stealing, and once again promise to give it up.

In writing up the girl's psychological history, Dr. Lorand pointed out that the injustices and deprivations of her early life, the "miseries which had driven her to consolation in fantasy," and her constant thought that nobody loved her, contributed to her need to steal. She felt she had been cheated from childhood on.

"Since it is plain that her complaint was based on reality, we must grant its right to existence," said Dr. Lorand. "To the child, human beings are the only constituents of his life who tell lies, and even people as highly admired as parents have that weakness. This was certainly true in the case under discussion, in which the mother, who played the role of both parents in the child's life, was always evasive and never told her the truth about what was to the child the most important of all matters—her father. Her character formation developed along this line, and attached to the major symptom of kleptomania was the minor one, consisting of an attempt to cheat and lie. *As far back as she remembered, demands had been put on her and nothing given in return, not even the mother's frankness* [italics are Dr. Lorand's]."

He also pointed out that the average child's sacrifices are equalized by certain compensations, usually taking the form of love from parents and teachers. But in this girl's case, compensation was almost altogether lacking. In her case, and in all cases of kleptomania, he said, stealing may be the result of a failure to achieve the wish to be loved—a wish which, according to Freud, plays a greater role in a girl's life than a boy's.

The root of female kleptomania must be sought, Dr. Lorand said, in the woman's desire to be a man. When the girl in this case stole, unconsciously the stolen object represented the penis she felt had once been stolen from her (little girls believe they were born with a penis, just like boys, but that it was taken from them). Kleptomania in women is considered the female counterpart to male fetishism, Dr. Lorand stated. In fetishism an object such as a shoe or a fur piece is used to symbolize the penis.

In this woman's life, both parents had failed to give her love or to set high moral standards for her, Dr. Lorand pointed out. The father had left his wife and daughter when the latter was only nine months old and from then on showed no interest in either of them. The girl, as she grew up, knew she had a father in America, but felt that he did not really care about her or her mother. She also held her mother responsible for her father's desertion, for children often blame the mother when the father abandons the home.

"The symbolic meaning of this kleptomania was the obtaining by force what she had been unable to get in a natural way—the love of her parents," said Dr. Lorand. "Kleptomania means the gain of something, the having it in one's possession. *The action of stealing is a displacement and represents another action around the Oedipus situation—taking love* [italics Dr. Lorand's]."

Dr. Lorand pointed out that is why, in kleptomania, "the stolen object has no value to the offender; it is the action and not the result which gives pleasure."

At the start of treatment, the girl denied she had any sexual feelings whatsoever. If, at times, a quite transparent sexual dream occurred, she would ignore it, although she did grant that the dream was the fulfillment of a wish. She never gave a thought to sex, she told Dr. Lorand (he noted she had a good figure and was attractive). She could not recall that she had ever masturbated in childhood, an act normal to most children. Stealing had evidently replaced sexual pleasure by the time she was adolescent, Dr. Lorand said.

"This asexual attitude was obviously superficial; behind it there was the strong craving for love and the lack of gratification drove her to compensation, which she derived from her stealing," Dr. Lorand summed up.

As treatment progressed, she was able to face her deep fear of sex and realize the stealing had been one symptom of it.

After the young woman's treatment ended, Dr. Lorand lost track of her until a few years later, when he met her father. The latter reported that she had been living away from home for more than a year, was working in an office and had both men and women friends. She visited him and his wife occasionally, and seemed, on the whole, much happier.

# "None So Blind"

Psychoanalytic treatment has even been extended to the person known as the criminal psychopath. The late Robert Lindner, a psychologist, used what he called "hypnoanalysis" as a means of exploring the unconscious mind of a young criminal. Dr. Lindner wrote about this experience in *Rebel Without a Cause* (published by Grune & Stratton in 1944; later became a movie which bore no relation to the book except for the title).

The technique of hypnoanalysis enabled Dr. Lindner to take the youth he called Harold back to his childhood, then to earliest infancy. He was able eventually to recall scenes he saw from his crib when he was between six and eight months old.

This study illustrated once again the validity of many of Freud's theories. It showed the nature of "displacement"—the young man had violently assaulted and tried to kill an older man whom he admitted reminded him strongly of his father. This man had called Harold obscene names which had enraged him because they represented some of his deepest, most dangerous wishes.

The book also dramatically showed how traumatic it may be for a baby to witness parents having sexual intercourse. At the time, a baby does not know exactly what is happening. But it will become frightened and the experience leaves what psychoanalysts call a memory trace which may later affect his sexual and aggressive feelings.

The study also showed how direct the relationship may be between repressed emotions of fear and guilt and a physical symptom. It demonstrated too how the unwitting, partial seduction of a child by a parent may lead to later violence in the child.

The method of hypnoanalysis, in which the person is first lightly hypnotized, then gradually placed in deeper and deeper trances until finally he does not even feel a lighted cigarette against his skin, is not accepted by most psychoanalysts as a valid method of treatment. In this case, it was primarily used for research, although a strong feeling of trust developed on the part of Harold toward his therapist, and Dr. Lindner maintained that the young man was helped through the understanding he gained of the early conflicts that led to his life of crime.

Dr. Lindner looked on hypnoanalysis as "a psychotherapeutic technique of promise," one that speeded up the classical process of analysis. Because of the death of Dr. Lindner, there has been no further report on what happened to Harold. However, we learn in the book that the pronounced physical eye tic and poor vision from which he had suffered since childhood improved considerably.

As a result of his study of Harold and other criminals, Dr. Lindner concluded that the psychopath was emotionally still a child bent on achieving instantaneous gratification of his every wish, no matter how much it hurt him or others. Psychopathy, in essence, he said, was a prolongation of infantile patterns and habits into the stage of physiological adulthood.

Dr. Lindner further stated he believed the psychopath never progressed beyond the pregenital level of sexual development (concern with the self) to the stage where he could love someone else. The experiences of his early life fixated his sexual energy, what Freud called "libido," before the adult, or genital level, was reached. This, coupled with his demand for instant satisfaction of every desire, accounted for his many, haphazardly chosen sexual partners whom he promptly abandoned, as well as for the primitive violence in which he often engaged. Dr. Lindner also noted the intense egotism of the psychopath, just like the child's.

Without the use of hypnoanalysis, Harold undoubtedly would not have been able to plumb the depths of his unconscious. Therapy or no, this case is a landmark in research. It is probably one of the deepest explorations yet made of a man's unconscious.

¶While studying a number of criminal psychopaths in a prison in an eastern state, Dr. Lindner, at the urging of one of his clinical assistants, sent for Harold, a young man of twenty-one. The assistant felt some of Harold's symptoms should be studied and treated.

Prison records showed that the young man's criminality began at the age of twelve when, with some other boys, he broke into a grocery store and helped rob it of $75 worth of candy and tobacco. He was sent to a juvenile institution for examination, where he tried to escape by leaping through a window. Caught, he was placed on two years' probation. At thirteen he was arrested for trespassing, and his probationary period extended. At fifteen he stole a large sum of money from a storekeeper and probation was resumed. A month later, he bought a rifle and tried to rob a couple sitting in a car on a lonely city street. The man managed to disarm him and hold him for the police. Again Harold went to juvenile court and was put on probation for five years. Once he received a short sentence to a correctional institution for breaking and entering a house. Several similar charges were pending when he was arrested for stabbing a man. It was a crime serious enough to carry a heavy penalty.

Harold was Roman Catholic and spent the fourth to seventh grades in a parochial school after attending public school for the first three years. He left the parochial school to become a pupil in a special class for students with defective vision. At fifteen he graduated to high school, which he quit after a year. He gave up all attempts at study and worked sporadically on a relative's farm while looking in vain for a job. He would always fail the eye tests.

His father, a machinist by trade, was an unnaturalized Pole who had come to the United States at the turn of the century. He met and married an American-born girl and they settled in an industrial suburb of a large eastern city. Their first child was Harold; two years later a daughter was born, and then another daughter several years later. The father fell ill with an occupational disease which forced him to give up his job in a factory. He then worked on his own at various jobs, usually using his ability as a machinist. His average earnings were $25 a week. Investigators described him as a disciplinarian more ready with curses and cruel words than blows, although Harold gave many examples of physical blows dealt him by his father over the years. His father did not smoke or drink.

Harold's mother appeared to be a worn and tired woman, harassed by the daily drudgery of bringing up a family on little money. They lived in a four-room apartment, for which they paid $12 a month. It was above a saloon in an old building in a run-down but respectable neighborhood.

The mother reported Harold's birth as normal and his childhood as healthy, except for an attack of measles at the age of two, after which his eyes started their blinking. She took him to doctors over the years, who found nothing physically wrong with his eyes and were unable to help him. He had 10 per cent normal vision in the right eye and 15 per cent in the left.

The many psychologists and psychiatrists who examined and tested Harold, while disagreeing as to what caused his life of crime, all agreed on a diagnosis of psychopathic personality complicated by social difficulties stemming from the condition of his eyes. One psychiatrist reported the presence in Harold of "a subconscious jealousy of the father and a mother fixation." Another found Harold honest and fairly intelligent and, questioning him closely on his sexual practices, obtained an admission of masturbation and sexual relations with girls in the neighborhood from the age of eight on. Harold had an I.Q. of 107.

Dr. Lindner's first impression of Harold was of a fairly tall, sparely built boy with wide shoulders and narrow hips. His face was rather intelligent. At times he rose and paced the room with what Dr. Lindner called the curious litheness and agility common to psychopaths. The one feature that attracted immediate attention was his heavy-lidded, continually fluttering eyes, which gave his face the almost masklike appearance of the totally blind, unless the observer noticed the restless, shifting play of the pupils and the fast blinking of the lids.

Although Harold at first seemed sneering and sullen, saying he did not think treatment would do him any good, he agreed to take part in the experiment with the new therapy. In answer to Dr. Lindner's question as to whether he would rather be blind than become able to keep his eyes open for longer periods, Harold replied, "I'd rather be blind than to see some of the things I have seen."

He entered the trance state rapidly and easily, obeying all instructions. In response to the suggestion that his lids stay open and remain fixed and steady while a strong light was directed into his eyes, Harold, who did not recall looking into daylight with his eyes open and for whom an electric light was a stimulus to rapid blinking, opened his eyes and stared directly into the sharp light. This convinced him, Dr. Lindner wrote, that Harold's condition, although essentially physical, had been initiated by a traumatic psychological assault on the boy at a crucial stage in his very early development.

There were recorded, in all, over a microphone concealed in the couch on which Harold lay, forty-six sessions. The microphone was connected with a loudspeaker in another room where a stenographer took down everything that was said.

During the first few sessions, Harold discussed life at the prison and general topics such as the current politics and marriage. He stated that he didn't think he would get married because when a man married he put a big obstacle in his way, and no great man in history had ever wished to marry. Dr. Lindner commented that such remarks were a standard sign of psychopathy, showing an inability to accept social or personal responsibility.

During the third session, Harold mentioned his father. He said he hardly ever spoke to him because they never got along. He recalled that once, when he was thirteen, his mother told him to call his father, who was busy fixing tires in the garage, in to supper and his father picked up a hammer and threatened to hit him with it.

Harold also remembered that when he was fifteen his father and mother had quarreled and his father had struck his mother, knocking her to the floor. Harold picked up an iron poker and was about to hit his father with it but his sister pulled it out of his hands.

When he was a boy he joined a gang that stole bicycles, cars, food—everything, he said, that was not nailed down. Sometimes they set fires in empty houses. Most of the boys had rifles and knives they had stolen. He got into countless fights with boys who taunted him because of his eyes. He said he thought people did not like him because his eyes blinked so, and when they made remarks about his eyes he felt like choking them with his hands and hitting their heads against the side of a building.

He often played hookey from school, staying away from home four and five days at a time. Sometimes his father would hit him when he returned, sometimes his mother. His father resented Harold's inability to get a job. He, too, taunted Harold about his eyes. (In a later session Harold recalled his father had once called him "a blind bat" in Polish.) When his father hit him, he would put up his hands to protect his eyes. In school the teachers would punish him by putting him in a back seat where he could not see the blackboard and so he never did any work.

His mother, grandmother, and sister made him go to church even though he hated it and he would try to find some excuse for not going. One Sunday morning he and his cousin Emma were left alone in the house when everyone else went to church and he kissed Emma and played with her breasts. In subsequent sessions he spoke of much sexual play with young girl cousins and girl neighbors, as well as of several attempts at seduction by a young aunt.

During the tenth session, Harold informed Dr. Lindner that his eyes had improved and everyone in prison to whom he talked had noticed it. He could open them much wider and they didn't blink as much, even in the sunlight. During the eleventh session, Harold spoke of his longing for sex while in prison. Throughout the sessions, he mentioned his closest friend in the jail, Perry, who tried constantly to seduce him into a homosexual affair. Harold never gave in, although he said he had considered it because he enjoyed Perry's company and did not want to lose his friendship. He compared Perry to his mother in that they both had a pitiful, helpless look. He told Dr. Lindner he had been sexually involved with a man only once.

Threaded throughout the remaining sessions were recollections of the many beatings he got from his father. Once he was beaten for taking his father's razor and cutting wood off his bureau. He said his mother was usually kind to him even though she occasionally beat him, too. But she would stand up for him when his father ridiculed him. When he wanted money he would throw his arms around her, kiss her, and tell her how young and beautiful she looked and she would give it to him. She would also give him money to go to movies so he would be out of his father's way when the latter came home from work.

During the twentieth session, Harold remarked that he had always believed, since he was ten, that when he reached twenty-one he would either be dead or his eyes would be fixed. He told Dr. Lindner he was just past twenty-one, not dead, and his eyes were getting better. At the next session he described the brutality of a priest in the parochial school who struck the pupils so hard with his cane that once a boy collapsed on the floor. During the following session, Harold explained that the reason he stole guns was that he liked the noise, and he liked to feel the vibrations when the gun went off. He commented that when he carried a gun he thought he was better than other people. A gun, he said, gave him courage, backed him up, imbued him with a real feeling of manliness. He also liked to throw knives, he said.

During the next session he recalled seeing his mother partially nude in the bathtub in the middle of their kitchen, where everyone took baths. His mother always insisted that he wash her back. He said he did not like to do it but whenever he objected she would "swing around and hit me." Once he asked why she didn't get his sister to wash her back and she hit him and yelled, "You do what you're told!"

He remembered seeing his sister naked when she took baths. He also recalled that when he was about ten and his sister eight they would take naps on summer afternoons, encouraged by their mother, in what he called "a cradle . . . like a junior bed." At these times, he would fondle his sister all over. He remembered having intercourse with her five or more times.

At the next session he again mentioned disliking his father, then recalled as a boy hearing his parents at night in the next room preparing for intercourse. He hated to hear this and would cover his head with the blanket. During this session he also remembered that his father told him he was going to cut off his penis and give it to his sister, who was a tomboy. His father always said he wished Harold was the girl instead of his sister because she would fight anybody while he was afraid to fight. Once his father threatened to sic the dog Nellie on him, saying the dog would bite off his penis. His mother overheard and scolded his father for saying such a thing. She called the boy over, told him to pat Nellie on the head, and see that she would not bite him.

During the twenty-seventh session, Harold again spoke of his father, this time of the hairiness all over his body except for his balding head, and his large chest. He said his father looked like a big gorilla. Four sessions later, Harold, placed in a deep trance, spoke haltingly and with apparent strain of how his eyes always burned in the sunlight and how he liked to go out at night when they would stay open. He recalled his mother telling him that when she was first married his father beat her and she left him for several days. He also remembered that as a small boy he wore dresses and stayed close to his mother. There also came to mind a scene when, as a child, he had stepped on a nail and his aunt had called him in Polish "a blind dog."

The thirty-fifth hour yielded a goldmine as far as memory was concerned. He spoke of his eyes improving, saying he didn't know if there was anything wrong with them in the first place. Then he recalled a time when as a baby he had slept in a cradle with squared wooden bars which stood between a bureau and his parents' bed. The cradle was placed to the right of the bed. Often in the morning, after his father left for work, his mother would take him into bed with her. He remembered that, as a matter of habit when he awoke, he would look over to see if she was in bed or had gone to the kitchen.

Then, speaking with "much overt expression of pain and suffering," according to Dr. Lindner, Harold recalled an episode that related directly to his physical symptoms. He told again how he would wake up in the morning to see the sun shining into the room, then look over at his parents' bed to see if his mother was in it. If she was, he would make a noise so she would come over and pick him up.

But this one morning (it proved to be a Sunday) when he awoke, he looked at the bed; his parents were having intercourse. His mother saw him staring at them, said something to his father, and they got out of bed. He recalled seeing and being frightened of his father's genitalia because they were "big, so big." He compared them to "a vicious animal." He again mentioned the sun "shining, shining into the room," then spoke of his fear that his father had hurt his mother and would hurt him.

During the next session Harold, again in a deep hypnotic trance, confessed that he had murdered a man (as it turned out, the man lived but Harold believed at the time that he had killed him). He described how it happened. An older man who had spent time in jail, with whom he occasionally played cards, and who cheated, had been playing pool at a table next to him one night. Harold pulled his stick back to make a shot, and accidentally struck this man on the elbow. Harold remembered that the room was dark except for the lights above the table. The man asked why he didn't watch what he was doing, then cursed him. Harold apologized. The man called him "a lying mother-f - - - - r," and other obscene names. Harold told Dr. Lindner that he went home "agitated," saying he had often slept with his mother in the same bed until he was fifteen when she had fights with his father, but "I would never even touch her." He remained in a daze for about a week. Then he decided he would get even with this man. He caught up to him on the street one day, pulled out a hunting knife he had stolen a few years before from his father, and plunged the knife into the man's neck several times, then into his chest, and finally "way down." He left the man lying on the street, thinking he was dead.

At this point, Harold again recalled the morning he had seen his parents naked on the bed. He remembered how, after his mother had picked him up and placed him in the high chair in the kitchen, his father had looked "mad," his black eyes "shining" as though he wanted to hit him.

It was evidently at this very moment that Harold's eyes first started to become affected. He described sitting in the high chair, his father talking to him. He said, ". . . I don't understand what he is saying. I'm afraid of him . . . And his eyes, they look all lit up . . . I don't know what's the matter. I can see my father. There is still a light in his eyes. It is coming right at me, two little darts coming right at me. Before they were bright, now they are smaller. My mother—there are no lights in my mother . . . I can see my father's eyes, both of them. The light is coming at me now. It's going at my mother. It's cut off . . . The lights seem to be going in one ear and one eye—but—I don't know—what that is. I can't see anything else . . . Everything is black, blacker. The lights are moving in two rays. They're missing me. They're in front of me. I want—I want to go to her. It's black: I see nothing."

He went on to speak of two lights, turning, shining, hitting him, coming from where his father sat, like headlights on an automobile, two spotlights. He tried to duck, but they hit him and he was afraid. He held his hand up to his face. Then it turned black again. Then the lights flashed on, hurt his eyes so that he felt an ache in the back of his brain, as though someone had stuck a knife into his eyes.

Dr. Lindner asked why the lights were coming from his father's eyes. Harold replied that when he was lying in the cradle and saw his father on top of his mother, his mother looked at him and her eyes were soft and pitiful but his father's eyes were hard "like bright lights." He said he saw "the whites, looking right into my eyes, shining." Then he said, "I don't know whether I am afraid of his eyes or his penis more. They're mixed. His eyes—his penis . . ."

While Harold was still in a deep trance, Dr. Lindner asked him to remember back even before that Sunday morning. Harold recalled a time when he was about six months old and was drinking from a bottle with a nipple on it. His father sat near by, his eyes "having green in them but they were not shining." Only the sun was shining, and his own eyes were not blinking. The blinking started after he saw his father and mother having intercourse.

Then he spoke again of what he called his "accident," when he stabbed the man on the street. He said the man resembled his father in that he was strong, had a big chest, was "tough," and could have picked up Harold and dropped him on the floor, as his father had done when he was small. He said he thought maybe he was getting even with his father when he stabbed the man.

At the next session, the thirty-seventh, Harold mentioned thoughts of suicide after his assault. The following session, he recalled that when he was seventeen he planned to get rid of his father but could not bring himself to kill him, even though his father was so mean to him, because he did not want the responsibility of supporting his mother and two sisters. However, his plan to murder his father came to mind when he thought of killing the man who cursed him. His father, he said, had once called him a "blind bum" and a liar.

Dr. Lindner pointed out to Harold, at this time, that he himself had shown how, in attacking the man, he was, in reality, trying to kill his father. Then he asked Harold the origin of his hate for his father. Harold replied, "I—I . . . you know. That—what—I saw . . . My mother and my father . . . He was—hurting—her . . ."

34

Dr. Lindner further pointed out that the man in the pool room had accused Harold of doing the same thing Harold saw his father doing—having sexual intercourse with his mother. Dr. Lindner maintained that the man, by Harold's own admission, had reminded him of his father who, also by his own admission, he had wanted to get rid of so he could have his mother all to himself.

At this moment, Harold confessed he wanted to do something he had not done for a long time—cry—although he did not know why. He started to sob. For about ten minutes he was incoherent. (Such a reaction to a therapist's interpretation is indicative that the therapist has hit home.)

After Harold stopped crying Dr. Lindner asked if he felt better. Harold said he did, that he really didn't hate his father. He said he loved his mother and that was one reason he did not carry out his plan to kill his father. He told Dr. Lindner this was the first time in a long while that he felt relieved. His shoulders and arms felt lighter, he said.

During the following session Dr. Lindner started interpreting to Harold what had happened, as shown by his memories, his dreams, and his thoughts. Dr. Lindner mentioned the many times Harold spoke of moving to get out of the way of the "lights" in his father's eyes after seeing his parents in bed and imagining his father was hurting his mother (the way most children interpret the act of intercourse). When he saw his father's enormous (to him) penis, it was a sight difficult to bear, something alien and dangerous. Because Harold thought he was seeing something forbidden, which was confirmed by the furtive actions of his parents upon being discovered in the sex act, he felt extremely guilty. *He had seen something he should not have seen.* He feared the wrath of his father because he, the son, was an interloper. The "light" in his father's eyes was a look of anger, one he sought to avoid from then on.

Because of this experience, and, as Dr. Lindner pointed out, because "of the intrinsic character of your father, because of the kind of person he was"—a man who threatened to cut off his son's penis, a father who rejected and humiliated his son—Harold grew up hating his father and hating himself. (Dr. Lindner did not mention this, but Harold's mother also played her part in his emotional illness, practically leading him into incest with his sister and seducing him to a certain extent by insisting he wash her back while she lay naked in the bathtub.)

Harold had carried with him over the years his guilt at his wish to take his father's place with his mother, to substitute for his father, Dr. Lindner said.

At this point Harold declared that compared to his father in every way he was nothing, and that he was jealous of his father. But when he had a gun with him, he added, he didn't care what his father said to him, as he could always take care of him then.

Dr. Lindner reiterated that Harold had tried to kill a man who accused him of the very act he wanted to forget—his father engaging in intercourse with his mother, which was also Harold's hidden wish. Dr. Lindner said, "In a word, you really are what he called you." He also pointed out that Harold had used a knife, rather than a gun, because the knife was, for him, a symbolic representation of the penis. It was a knife he had stolen from his father as he might wish to steal his father's penis. He feared his father might take away his own penis, as he had threatened to do, because of his incestuous wishes for his mother. His many hurried sexual escapades were attempts to convince himself he was a man, that his father had not castrated him in retaliation for his wish to kill him and possess his beautiful young mother.

Harold had run away from what he had seen as a baby, sensing that it was forbidden and feeling frightened and guilty. He had run away by closing his eyes, Dr. Lindner told him. His whole life was a battle with his father, a running away from his father and his inadequate self. He wound up by trying to commit a symbolic murder that he thought would rid him of his father.

It was during the forty-first hour that Harold recalled another experience, one that fitted more of the pieces of his early life into place. He remembered what had happened the night before he saw his parents having intercourse. It had been a Saturday night and his mother and father had taken him to a movie. He recalled men with big hats, cowboys with guns, and a wolf or a dog (Rin-Tin-Tin, perhaps, Dr. Lindner suggested). Harold said that he half lay, half sat in his mother's arms during the movie.

He spoke of bright rays of light coming from the projection room and flashing on the screen—two separate rays. He saw the heads of men and women in the audience around him. He reached up to touch his mother and she put his hand down, intent on watching the movie. He saw more flashes of light from the projector in the back. He heard his father whisper to his mother. Light shone on his father's face. Then he saw light on the screen, showing the picture of a horse which opened its mouth and displayed big teeth. Turning his head, over his mother's shoulder he saw again the rays of light. They seemed to be shooting at him and he was frightened. Then the movie was over and he was once more in his carriage, his mother pushing it while his father walked on her left.

The next morning as he sat in the high chair, Harold said he saw once again the lights of the night before, this time as though glaring out of his father's eyes. His father's face looked "cut up" and also looked like the picture of a devil or a dog, with the ears sticking up and out. He started to cry. His mother picked him up, talked to him, and rocked him in her arms, his head on her left shoulder.

Three sessions later, Harold remarked that his eyes were a hundred per cent better. He said there was nothing really worrying him now, although he had a feeling "of a longing for loneliness." (He knew the sessions were nearing their end and was trying to hide his disappointment, Dr. Lindner explained.)

At the next to last session, Harold admitted he felt sorry for his father, who was then in a hospital with a fractured leg. At the final session, he said he had been thinking of all the things he and Dr. Lindner had talked about and realized they were connected. He again remarked his eyes were much better, in that the pupils were contracted, he could read small print, and they only blinked about half as much as before.

He asked Dr. Lindner to go over what had happened in the

previous forty-five sessions. Dr. Lindner explained to him that many of his difficulties went back to that traumatic morning and the night before when he was taken to the movies, both experiences new and frightening to a baby. Harold had remembered his father's face, lit up in the dark theater, and scenes from the movie which frightened him when he saw the wolf or dog. The next morning, when he saw something that he was dimly aware he should not see because his mother pushed his father away from her and pointed guiltily to Harold, he was afraid his father would hurt him. At the breakfast table he looked at his father (who was undoubtedly angry at being interrupted during sexual intercourse) and the shock of the night before became associated with his fear and hatred of his father. Dr. Lindner explained to Harold that to children that young all time becomes as one, with no sharp lines dividing day and night.

As a baby, Harold had started to cry when he saw the two rays of the night before from the projection room now streaming from his father's angry eyes. He saw his father's face all "cut up," as he had described the face of the dog in the movie (he had compared the sight of his father's penis to "a vicious animal").

Harold's blinking and his poor vision were associated with his fear relating to these two experiences, Dr. Lindner concluded. Harold had tried to escape the fear by closing his eyes, the guilty organs, for they had seen that which they were forbidden to see. He had tried to close his eyes forever to shut out the sight in bed that had caused him so much agony, jealousy, and guilt.

But the fear of his father and his father's big penis had followed him all through life. He stole guns and knives, trying to convince himself he had a penis, trying to prove himself as good a man as his father, but all the while his original dependence on his mother became greater.

His excessive masturbation was also a way of fighting his fear that his father would steal his penis, Dr. Lindner said, especially since his father had actually threatened to cut it off. Such a threat is a very serious one to a child, particularly when it follows a traumatic incident such as seeing parents having sex, and when parents themselves have deep emotional problems, Dr. Lindner said.

As the session neared its end, Harold admitted he understood that when he knifed the older man, he did it to try somehow to get rid of his father without really having to get rid of him. And that when he stole things and broke into houses, he was symbolically stealing his mother from his father.

In summarizing the case, Dr. Lindner declared that it offered a striking illustration of the truth of a remark made by the psychiatrist William A. White, that behind every criminal deed lies a secret. Dr. Lindner added that what is more important, however, is that "we have glimpsed the utter futility, the sheer waste, of confining individuals in barred and turretted zoos for humans without attempting to recover such secrets." He called Harold's case "a mockery of current penological pretense."

He pointed out that Harold plundered and almost killed in response "to those ungovernable needs which came flaring up from the deepest, remotest shafts of his being. Had he not undertaken analysis, all the trade-training, all the attentions of penal personnel would have been wasted on him; and like every other psychopath who leaves prison he would have been released again to the community as the same predatory beast who entered—with this exception: that his conflicts would have been driven more deeply and his hostility aggravated by a system that flatters itself that it is doing other than substituting psychological for physical brutality."

Dr. Lindner reported that during the sessions Harold had gained insight and a real understanding of the past and how it had affected his attitudes and goals. He not only saw better, but felt better and behaved better. Those who knew him commented on the change. Dr. Lindner concluded: "Gone is that sneering sullenness, that arrogant aggression, that Storm-Trooper mentality, that disregard for the rights and feelings of others. He knows that he was a psychopath: he knows why he was a psychopath: he knows that he needs to be a psychopath no more . . ."

# Marriages Are Made in Heaven

Is there a "contagious" aspect to emotional illness? May a child not "catch" emotional illness from his parents just as he would a physical disease?

Psychoanalysts believe that the very early emotional atmosphere, as well as the growing child's relationship to his parents, affects his psychological development. This, they say, explains why some survive psychologically while others become psychotic and fill our mental hospitals, even though all of us struggle with the same impulses and emotions.

What may happen between mother and child in the sense of "emotional contagion" is dramatically depicted in the following case history. The author is Dr. Alexander Gralnick, medical director of High Point Hospital in Port Chester, New York. He studied the family when he was on the staff of Central Islip State Hospital, Central Islip, New York. Originally appearing in *The Psychiatric Quarterly,* Vol. XVII (April 1943), it was titled "The Carrington Family: A Psychiatric and Social Study Illustrating the Psychosis of Association or *Folie à Deux.*"

The phrase "psychosis of association," which is Dr. Gralnick's, is more commonly referred to as *folie à deux.* In such instances, the two, three, or even four persons involved become so necessary to each other emotionally that they would rather destroy themselves than end the relationship. In Dr. Gralnick's words, "They are in dire need of each other."

A psychosis is a response to highly distorted human relationships, he says. "Mental illness does not grow out of something which lies solely within the affected person but is a result of the interplay of highly complex forces."

113

Today someone who catches a contagious physical disease that is known to be dangerous to others is quickly isolated and treated so that society will not suffer. Talking of the Carrington case, Dr. Gralnick commented, "We have been slow, however, to make this the common procedure with mental illnesses, despite the fact that they can be every bit as malignant in their social effects. There can be no doubt that early interference by some proper agency would have saved at least the two children."

¶A mother, father, and daughter were patients in Central Islip Hospital, all at the same time. Dr. Gralnick decided to find out if the facts of their lives revealed any possible connection among the emotional illnesses of the three members of this family.

The mother, whose maiden name was Anne Murphy, was born in London in 1890 of an Irish-Catholic mother and a German-Jewish father. She was the third child of this marriage. She thought of her father as a quiet man who had little to say and of her mother as a severe, domineering woman who showed little or no affection for her eleven children.

Anne recalled that at the age of fourteen when she began to menstruate, her mother's attitude changed toward her. She claimed her mother gave her poorer food than the rest of the children, banished her to an isolated room in the house, and turned her brothers and sisters against her. She said of the latter, "We were more like strangers; sometimes we would meet on the street, and they wouldn't take notice of me. I think it was my mother's fault. She got me in the habit of being alone, and I'd go upstairs to my room. I wasn't a favorite with her; she didn't like me. I know she didn't."

Anne said she was forced by her mother to go to work in a factory after she was graduated from elementary school with honors at twelve. She had wanted to remain in school, as her brothers and sisters were allowed to do, but her mother insisted she go to work, which confirmed Anne's suspicions that her mother disliked her.

She was introverted and seclusive, and did not try to make friends. After her day in the factory she went home and read. She became very interested in palmistry and dream interpretations. Once a fortune teller told her she would "marry a man from across the sea."

This prophecy came true in 1911, when she was twenty-one. One day she was stopped on the London streets by a sailor in the United States navy who asked directions. He told her that he was on a forty-eight hour shore leave, that his name was Cameron Carrington, that he was thirty-four-years old, and had been born in the British West Indies. His father, Thomas, a college graduate, had been a chemist-pharmacist until his business failed. At this time Cameron, the oldest of four children, was forced to leave private school. His mother, he said, was the "quiet" type.

Cameron, who unlike Anne, made friends easily, became a salesman in a general store in the British West Indies. When he was twenty-three, he joined the United States navy. After four years in the navy he went to work in New York as a streetcar conductor. He was fired after a year, following an accident involving his car, and rejoined the navy. When he met Anne in London she seemed, according to him, "amiable, happy, pleasant in her ways, and the athletic type."

He proposed immediately, declaring that he wanted to marry her when he returned to London. During his short leave, they "saw the sights." They also spent time in Anne's home, where he observed that his future mother-in-law was a good housekeeper.

Ten minutes after she met him, Anne said, she decided Cameron would be her husband. She believed marriages were arranged in heaven—that marriage was more or less a matter of fate. And had not the fortune teller predicted she would marry a man from across the sea?

Her mother urged her to get married, and pointed out that Anne might just as well marry Cameron as anyone else. If Anne had been able to choose, rather than believing marriage was something out of her control, she said she never would have married him. She was not fond of him but believed she could "tolerate" him. She felt she did not want children.

When he returned to London they were married, and immediately left for America. No one shed a tear. Anne thought her mother was "nasty" to her, but pleasant to Cameron. She told her husband she was glad to leave London. (She wrote her mother only once in twenty-eight years; she described her mother's answer as "nasty and curt" and so she never wrote her again.)

Anne felt calm about going to a new country, because, she said, "Nothing seemed to excite me." Not even sex, for, she said she never got any pleasure from it and just tolerated her husband's advances. They found an apartment in a poor section of Brooklyn, and Cameron got a job with the same streetcar company that had fired him. His income from a sixteen-hour day was about $16 a week. For a time Anne looked for employment, but turned down the factory jobs offered her because she thought the work was too hard.

They were forced to move several times, finally settling on a rundown block west of Tenth Avenue in Manhattan. They both hated it, but Anne refused to look for another apartment even though Cameron thought they could afford better. In spite of her professed hatred for the Catholic Church, she chose an apartment next to a Catholic church which she could see through one window. They lived there eighteen years; as Anne said, "We were always going to move but never did."

Within a few months, Anne was pregnant. She was unhappy because, she said, she felt this "a terrible world" into which to bring children, but Cameron was elated, as he was fond of babies. The baby, a girl, died at the hospital an hour after birth. The doctor said he was sorry about the death of the baby, and to Anne this was an admission that he had "killed" the infant through his carelessness.

After that, she became even more secluded. Always suspicious and isolated, she ungraciously discouraged neighbors from visiting her. Cameron lost the few friends he had because she refused to allow them in the house.

She was jealous of the landlady's wealth and fine clothes. She also continually expressed her hatred of the color green "because it brought bad luck" and represented the Catholic Church. She would not allow her husband to bring anything into the house if it was tied with green string. She would sit for hours, her head in her hands, staring into the fireplace. She said she could "see things" and predict the future, and she became outraged when her husband scoffed at her.

When her second daughter was born a year after the first child died, she slept with the new baby. She refused to have sexual intercourse until shortly before the conception of her son eight years later. She barred her bedroom door and would waken the baby if her husband gave signs of approaching her. After John was conceived, she avoided all intimacies despite her husband's repeated efforts during the next twelve years.

Edith, born in 1913, was a physically healthy baby who ate well and grew normally. She walked at nine months, talked at fifteen months. She was playful around the house and affectionate toward her father, who described her as "always laughing and full of energy." He taught her geography and the alphabet long before she went to school. At four she could read words from his newspaper.

Anne took pride in the baby and clothed her well, even sewing some of her dresses by hand. But she was overprotective, and carried her in her arms a great deal when the child should have been walking.

After Edith's birth, Cameron felt that his wife became exceedingly domineering and that she picked on him and made fun of him constantly. She forbade him to smoke. She threw away clothes he bought for himself. Finally he allowed her to buy everything, simply handing her his pay envelope. At first he objected when she served the same meals all the time, but then decided to say nothing.

Edith's troubles began when she was two, according to the record. She fell against a bedpost and cut her forehead, after which she started to squint, but her mother refused to have the child's eyes examined until five years later. By that time she needed an operation and had to wear glasses from then on.

Anne never let Edith go out by herself, and she was allowed to play with other children only in her mother's presence. After Edith was accidentally scratched on the face by a neighbor's child she was not allowed to play with the other children at all.

She was kept out of school by her mother until she was nine, at which time the school authorities threatened to take Anne to court unless she placed her daughter in school. In spite of her hatred of the Roman Catholic Church, Anne chose to send Edith to the Sacred Heart Catholic School because she felt the children there "were better behaved." Edith earned almost all A's in her first two years of school.

When Edith was eight, in 1921, Anne gave birth to John. She then turned all her attention to him, neglecting Edith for the most part. Cameron described his wife as "actually worshiping" her son. He said he had no doubt but that she became even more disturbed after John's birth. She grew "lazy and stout." She rarely told the truth and became more and more suspicious, insisting that everybody in the house was her "enemy." She chased away people who casually stopped to talk in front of the house, accusing them of spying on her. She forced her husband to speak quietly for fear that the neighbors would overhear; she would allow no one to enter the apartment. She wrapped kitchenware and clothes in paper bags and refused to let anyone look inside them.

She read the Bible extensively, saying that it represented to her the one true religion, that of the Hebrews. She was "a great lover of Jesus," loving him, she said, because he saved people from going to hell by his own suffering. She read to her children from the Book of Revelations and often predicted the world would come to an end.

She slept with John from the time of his birth until shortly before he died in his eighteenth year. She would often sit up until two or three in the morning by his side before going to sleep. To her, John was "a beautiful baby," full of life and spirit. At nine months he walked and, soon after, talked. He too was a very bright child, and when he went to public school at six he received almost all A's and B's.

As had been true with Edith, Anne watched John's every step. She had read in the Bible that Mary Magdalene washed Jesus' feet, and every day without fail Anne washed her son's feet, even though it often made him late for school. She did this almost to the day he died. Although at first he objected, John learned to submit to her ritual of feet washing.

She would not allow John to play with other children, just as she had never allowed Edith. He could do nothing without his mother's permission. Although at first he occasionally disobeyed, he eventually gave in to her. He read a lot and became a bookworm, like his sister.

At times Anne forbid her children to talk to their father, telling them he was their "enemy." At first Edith refused, and threatened to run away, but after a while she merely retreated to a corner and sat in silence.

As children Edith and John became allies and were fond of each other. When their mother was busy, they played harmonicas and sang, cut out paper toys, tossed a ball against the bedroom wall, or read.

Because of her suspicions and fears, Anne walked Edith to school every day. When Edith was pushed down the steps by another child and suffered a broken tooth, Anne took her out of school at once. She claimed that the nuns were "turning the other children against Edith," and she destroyed all the report cards Edith had received from the school.

About this time, Edith recalled, Anne also began to think that the Catholic Church was "against" her. She kept telling her daughter that Cameron had sent her to the parochial school, although in reality she was the one who had chosen it.

As the children grew up, Cameron worked in several places, including a pickle factory, where he put up orders for truckmen to deliver. He began to notice the gaiety of the girls in the factory as compared to his wife's morose behavior, which, he said, was driving him "nutty."

When he was at home at night he heard the voices of the girls at the factory singing. He imagined that he was being watched by the young girls in the neighborhood and that during the day they talked about him and laughed at him. He recalled that Anne had said that people talked about them, and, in fact, she would frequently go to the door to see if people were standing outside listening.

For no apparent reason, he started to cry at times. He heard voices threatening Anne and himself with death. While he was in the hospital he described these experiences: "The gang that is after me is trying to burn out my sexual organs with rays coming through the ceiling. I woke up and found my glands all heated up." He heard voices ordering unseen enemies to shoot him.

He became so beset with hallucinations that, in 1928, he was committed to Central Islip State Hospital, one of New York State's large mental hospitals. Helped by a psychiatrist, he came to realize that the voices he thought he heard were imaginary. He said he believed his wife's strange behavior was the cause of his troubles. After a year he was discharged. On his return, Anne became even more insistent that the children not talk to their father. She said he was "crazy," and if they spoke to him they too would become insane.

Edith and John continued to get good marks in school. In spite of her late start, Edith was graduated from junior high school at fourteen. She entered Haaren High School in 1928, and for the first term her grades dropped to B's. But at this point, with her father hospitalized, her mother took her out of school and insisted that she go to work.

The Charity Organization Society helped the family financially when Edith could not find a job and returned to school. But now she did poorly and at seventeen she gave up and was released by the school at her request. From then on she stayed home and never once looked for work.

John, whose I.Q. was recorded at 123, was graduated from public school with excellent ratings in "reliability, leadership, civic spirit, industry and good manners." He received many prizes, for his marks were high. His English teacher noted that he was "a splendid student, but obviously suffering from some inner disturbance which revealed itself in extreme shyness and sensitivity." On his history record was written, "The boy has such an inferiority complex that he makes a poor impression in spite of his ability."

The children were denied any sex education by their parents— the subject of sex was taboo—and both said they would never marry or have children. Edith, at twenty-one, and John, at thirteen, promised each other that they would always stay together, that John would take care of Edith when she was old.

They shuddered at the frequent quarrels between their mother and father. John would shrink from his mother's touch when she tried to pat him on the shoulder as she helped him on with his coat. At times, sullen and angry with her, he sided with his father over her objections. Although Anne considered him "stubborn and self-willed," she always wanted him near her. She said she thought he disliked girls.

Cameron got a job with a plumber after his discharge from the hospital in October 1929, and worked regularly, despite the depression, until 1932. He was accepted for the WPA but after several years, in 1935, was dropped from the rolls because he was not a citizen—his eight years in the United States navy did not count. The New York City Department of Public Welfare then helped the family, although Cameron continued to try to find work. The best he could get was an occasional odd job. He spent hours in the park reading the paper and talking to strangers in order to avoid going home where no one spoke to him.

He found Anne more and more unbearable. At times he struck her in the face, which he had never done before. He brooded about his unemployment. He began to believe that the Catholic Church was behind all his troubles, as his wife insisted. Again he heard voices. He felt that a gang was after him, at Anne's instigation, threatening his life and accusing him of sexual degeneracy.

Once Cameron thought he smelled poison gas. He became so

dizzy that he had to open the windows and breathe fresh air. He became so fearful of "enemies" that he kept a hammer by his side. He used it one night to beat a drunken man mercilessly because he thought he heard the man make derogatory remarks about his sexual habits. At this time he voluntarily went for help to Bellevue Hospital on the advice of the police. He was readmitted to Central Islip in 1939, ten years after his discharge.

Meanwhile Anne's behavior was growing more violent. One night she walked into the dining room carrying a butcher knife and told her husband that she was going to kill him. She wrapped the knife in a paper bag and hid it. Another time she read of a woman killing her husband with a rolling pin, went out and bought one, and threatened to kill Cameron with it. She dressed in the same dirty clothes around the house that she slept in at night. She wore a hat and coat indoors even in hot weather and "plugged cotton in her ears" to keep them warm. She insisted that Edith and John do the same. John refused, but Edith obeyed her mother.

The apartment became a pigsty. The rooms, with their grimy, sooty walls, were littered with rubbish, tin cans, stacks of old newspapers, and paper bags. Anne would not clean the place nor allow anyone else to do so. Window panes were broken and pipes leaked, but she would not let a plumber in to repair the pipes. Once she permitted the rooms to be painted, but only after the landlord forced his way in with the painters.

The children grew thin and sallow. They had lost all initiative and were completely dominated by their mother. She complained of backaches and trouble in walking, and for a whole year she stayed indoors, refusing even to shop. At this time, Edith's hands became numb and her arms weak so that her mother had to cut her meat for her. Repeatedly Anne told welfare investigators that "all the young are better off dead due to the condition of the world today."

About two months before his father's return to the mental hospital, John refused to eat very much and started to lose weight, and talked hardly at all. He went to school regularly, however, until his mother told him that Cameron's strange talk and actions meant Cameron was "going off again." Then John stayed home, saying he did not feel well.

When his father went once again to the mental hospital, John fell into a complete decline. He either sat in a chair all day, refusing to move, or paced up and down the house. He suffered seizures of abdominal pain and vomiting. He lost his temper with his mother, chasing her "with a wild look in his eyes," according to a neighbor. Often Anne ran out into the hall to escape his wrath, and he would slam the door shut after her. She explained his outbursts by saying he was born under the sign of Taurus and had "the temper of a bull."

At this time a social worker who visited the home for the Welfare Department described John as "a morbid, silent boy, who barely said yes or no." She thought that he was "ill of starvation." In spite of Anne's protests, the social worker called a doctor, who recommended immediate hospitalization. Over his mother's objections, John was taken to Metropolitan Hospital. There he was diagnosed as suffering from "mixed hysterical psychoneurosis," with "emphysema over the entire chest." His electrocardiogram showed evidence of heart damage.

Anne visited her son in the hospital and asked him to show her his palm. Examining it, Anne explained to Edith, in front of him, that his lifeline was broken and he might not live. She had seen "the sign of death" in his hand, she said, and therefore would take him home. She commented without emotion that it was too bad John had to die.

She demanded that the hospital release him, and the doctors assented, seventeen days after his admission. A social worker who visited the home shortly after his return, saw him "lying on a pile of rags on one of the bedsprings, the dirt and grime so thick on his body that it could have been scraped off any part of him." No longer did his mother wash his feet. He ate little, said nothing.

Anne told the janitress, "My boy is crazy. He's lying down on the floor. He and his father are both mad."

A few weeks after his return, he refused to eat at all for two days. His mother and sister discussed calling a doctor but never did, although they got John ready for an ambulance. During his last night, John's breathing became heavy and labored. His mother and sister sat side by side on the bed near him all night, but Anne would not look at her dying son. Early in the morning he stopped breathing. Edith touched her brother and found him stone cold. She placed her hand over his mouth, felt no breath. Anne said, "He must be dead." She did not cry. Edith shed a few tears but stopped when Anne told her to call the janitress. When the latter wanted to pray over John's body, Anne forbade her to do so.

The medical examiner listed the cause of death as "bronchopneumonia and exhaustion psychosis." John weighed eighty pounds.

Edith's life was now empty except for the domination and continual reprimands of her mother. She ate little and ceased menstruating. In February 1940 the two women were found by the social worker in a cold, darkened apartment clad in hats, coats, and robes. Edith lay on the bed, "blue and cold." A doctor summoned by the social worker predicted that "Edith will go the same as John if she and her mother are allowed to remain together at home."

The floor leading from the kitchen to the bedroom had been covered with rusty nails laid end to end in orderly fashion. The social worker was not allowed to cross until Anne had swept them aside, muttering, "spies and Jews."

On March 1, 1940, Anne and her daughter were taken to Bellevue. Both were then transferred to Central Islip State Hospital, which now housed all three members of the Carrington family.

Together in a ward for cooperative patients, the two women clung to each other, as they had at home. They sat in the same chair, which gave them a view of the corridor. Whenever they heard any attendant or official coming Anne would peek out to see who was there, and they would stop talking when someone entered the room. The hospital report indicates that they acted like children caught at the jam closet, warning each other of an enemy's approach.

"In all their actions, one thing was outstanding—complete domination of Edith by her mother," Dr. Gralnick stated. "This was noted by everyone who had contact with them, and was variously characterized as, 'Edith never talks when her mother is around,' 'her mother always answers for her,' 'when the mother says eat frankfurters, Edith eats frankfurters,' and 'Edith doesn't think for herself.' Reticence, seclusiveness, and suspiciousness were not their only similarities. Both carried their possessions with them; and when they slept, it was with a sheet wrapped over and around their heads, so that, lying in adjoining beds, one was the image of the other. Both lacked initiative, but could be stimulated to talk and work." They did a little cleaning and sewing.

Anne then began having delusions about the attendants. She thought that everyone who asked her to do something was Catholic. She accused social workers and the church of tricking her into entering the hospital. When her husband visited her from another ward, she charged him with being her enemy and of wanting to have her hanged. She said to Edith in his presence, "Didn't I always say he was my enemy? I always told you he was. He was my husband but that didn't stop him from being my enemy." Edith nodded agreement.

The two women were separated a few months after their admission. Away from her mother, Edith started to change. She made several friends, explaining, "I am not shy now. I have more confidence. I have more things to talk about and can carry on a conversation better." She said she wanted to go to work to support her parents when she left the hospital.

Within nine months she gained thirty pounds and started menstruating again, but the initial physical examination had shown that she was suffering from anemia and multiple sclerosis. At the hospital she became progressively more ill. Finally, she could not even visit her mother, who was housed in another building. Her vision became blurred, and she was so spastic she could hardly walk without support. She complained of dizziness and a pressure in her head when she bent over. But in spite of her physical handicaps, she continued to become more outgoing.

The study of this family ended in April 1942. The mother remained suspicious and paranoid, although her behavior was good and she required no special supervision. Occasionally her husband, who by then was discharged, visited her. Edith seemed outwardly the same, discussing her life freely, but saying she was mentally well and never should have been hospitalized. She seemed calm and fatalistic about her life as a whole.

In discussing the case, Dr. Gralnick points out that, as children, both Edith and John "were very healthy and bright." Because of her own unhappy childhood in which she received little love from her mother, Anne grew into a suspicious, hostile woman who felt isolated and afraid in a world haunted by imaginary enemies. As Dr. Gralnick put it: "Life became a struggle in which she could only survive by escaping from or dominating others so that they could not harm her." In some ways she was dependent upon her family, ". . . her reign depended on their slavish support and acquiescence. She needed them—to believe her sane, and to aid her in her general terror. She had, therefore, to keep them weak and under her control. Without their sustenance, Anne would have been completely alone and would have broken down long before.

"In the family situation which she created and maintained, such a person as Anne could be nothing but an evil force . . . instead of satisfying the human needs of her family, she distorted and destroyed them."

Edith developed what Dr. Gralnick called "morbid dependency," choosing to enter the world of psychosis with her mother rather than face the fact her mother was crazy and she would lose her. Cameron chose to go insane rather than lose his wife and children. John chose to die rather than face the psychic terror of his life.

# To Be or Not To Be—
# In Darkest Africa

Those who live in the cities of so-called civilized societies are prone to assume that such a complex and sophisticated art-science as psychoanalysis has application only to them. That this is not so is illustrated by a revealing psychoanalytic study of a witch doctor from Rhodesia. Written by the late Dr. Wulf Sachs, it was published in 1947 as *Black Anger* (later retitled *Black Hamlet* by Little, Brown & Co.).

The primary aim of the book, according to Dr. Sachs, was to collect dreams and fantasies and explore the workings of one primitive unconscious mind.

*Black Anger* is a unique account of the psychoanalysis of John Chavafambira, an African medicine man, sometimes called witch doctor. It proves that whether a man is born in the remote savanna or the heart of the world's largest city, he still faces the same unconscious conflicts when trying to separate himself from his parents and establish his own identity.

The book also reveals how similar—as Freud had pointed out earlier—are the fantasy worlds of primitive man, the child, and the psychotic. The African, heir to tribal taboos, superstitions, and belief in magic, as well as a traditionally long oral dependency on the mother (approximately one and a half to two years of breast feeding), has a particularly difficult time in maturing emotionally.

Dr. Sachs, born in Russia, became a citizen of the Union of South Africa, residing in Johannesburg. He got his medical degree at the Psychoneurological Institute in Leningrad, then studied for German, English, and South African degrees. He was a member of the British and International Psychoanalytical Societies and president of the South African Psychoanalytical Society. His other books include *Psychoanalysis and Its Practical Applications, The Insane African, Psychology of Nationalism,* and he wrote critiques of Hamlet, Dostoevski, Wassermann, Proust, and John Steinbeck. He was also editor and publisher of a fortnightly South African review, *The Democrat.*

¶Dr. Sachs was a psychoanalyst who also practiced regular medicine in Johannesburg. He saw private patients in his office and was on the staff of a mental hospital for the "blacks," where he discovered that insanity, in its cause, form, and content, was the same in both blacks and whites. This discovery made him eager to investigate the inner workings of the black man's mind in its normal state.

His chance came when he was called by a friend, a woman anthropologist conducting studies in South Africa, to treat a crippled African woman who suffered from excruciating pains in her legs. Dr. Sachs found this woman's husband, John, to be a very intelligent medicine man. He asked John if he would be willing to visit his office every day, five days a week, lie down on his couch, and speak freely as if he were thinking aloud. John consented. He was analyzed for a period of two-and-a-half years, with minor interruptions.

The fact that John was a witch doctor as well as an African added interest to the study, for to Dr. Sachs "witch doctor" meant a romantic, mysterious figure supposed to possess supernatural powers over good and evil. However, the sensational stories about African witch doctors that appeared in tabloids were largely a product of the imagination, Dr. Sachs stated, adding that the occasional misuse of power by medicine men, called "ngangas" (herbalists), was no more "heinous" than that of which white doctors were sometimes guilty.

John had no real knowledge of magic roots or secret brews. He used the same root for every disease; only the ritual of its preparation and administration differed. He was a diviner of the future and a dispenser of herbs. He told fortunes and provided medicines to guard against illness and ward off bad luck. He gave his fellow sufferers a belief in better luck, and it was this belief that acted as a consolation and an inspiration for overcoming life's hardships, Dr. Sachs said.

The author was struck by the fact that most of John's medicines were used for "love sickness" rather than for physical ills. John was known to possess the gift of settling quarrels between husbands and wives, for giving love philters.

Far from discouraging John from practicing his profession, Dr. Sachs said he encouraged him to continue. Dr. Sachs maintained that as long as the African is kept uneducated, starved, and diseased, he will need the medicine man's magic. All he did was to try to increase John's efficiency by giving John some of the white man's medical knowledge.

John had inherited his calling from his ancestors. Dr. Sachs noted that anything connected with medicine was dear to John's heart, that he was "a born doctor," with a compassion for all who suffered and a desire to help them.

His grandfather, Gwerere, had been a famous practitioner of the art handed down to him from his own father and grandfather. John's father had also been a well-known doctor and rich in cattle, goats, and land. John's paternal aunt, his father's only sister, had followed the same profession, and his mother, Nesta, was known far beyond the borders of her village, to have been chosen by the ancestral spirits to be their intermediary with the living. John remembered his mother being periodically seized by fits (obviously epileptic, said Dr. Sachs). Her body stiffened, her limbs twitched, her eyes opened wide, her pupils stared into space, white foam appeared on her mouth, and a few drops of blood trickled down her chin. Everyone knew that at such times the dead, the "midzimu," came down to talk to her and deliver messages. When the fit ended, signifying that the spirits had settled in her body, although faint and sleepy she would talk to the crowd that eagerly awaited her words. Through her second husband, Charlie, a medicine man, she would deliver the message, answer questions, and foretell the future.

When Dr. Sachs first visited John's wife, Maggie, John told him rather shyly and apologetically that his own medicines did not ease her pain. He suggested that some powerful poisoner was working against him (Africans believed, according to Dr. Sachs, that when anyone fell ill the cause was never to be found in his body but rather that someone had poisoned him). Or else, said John, his wife's sickness was due to her living among white people, in which case his medicines could not help. He said to Dr. Sachs, "I hear that you are a famous doctor. Please help my wife. She suffers so much."

As luck would have it, according to Dr. Sachs, he was able to relieve Maggie's pain. One day when she felt better, he stayed to talk to John, speaking as one doctor to another, and John felt flattered. Dr. Sachs offered to explain the white man's methods of treatment of diseases to him since he showed such great interest. Dr. Sachs told him that every good doctor had to have an understanding of people, know what they think, what they wish, why they are unhappy, and to do this, the doctor must first understand something of himself.

He then explained to John the theory of the unconscious and reported that John, no less than white people, was surprised by the thought that there were things within himself of which he was not aware. When Dr. Sachs offered to help John find out more about this secret part of himself, John agreed to learn. Dr. Sachs added that he later found out that John's real reason for cooperating in the analysis was his desire to learn about the white man's medicine so he would know more than his professional competitors, his uncle, Charlie, and his cousin, Nathan, on his return to the village where he was born and grew up. It was thus that the analysis began.

Their work together was carried out in an atmosphere of friendliness and mutual interest. Dr. Sachs was surprised at the medicine man's quick grasp of what was wanted of him and how freely he spoke, especially since John expressed a feeling of distrust of all white men; "Never trust a white man. We learn this in our cradle," he told Dr. Sachs. Contrary to the usual analytic procedure, Dr. Sachs wrote down everything John said. He quoted John as speaking normal English, rather than the broken but fluent English in which John talked, but his story remained unchanged in all details.

Dr. Sachs described John as a healthy man of thirty who stood nearly six feet tall and had strong muscles and purple-black skin. His facial expression was almost grim; his nose was "like the flattened beak of a hawk, and the mouth, thick and sensual, typical of his race."

John began his story at the time he left his native village, a village near Rusapi in Manyikaland, Rhodesia, and set out for the Union of South Africa. He was then about twenty. He decided to leave because he wanted to cut himself away from Charlie, his father's brother, who had become his stepfather when his father died (John was then six), as was the custom of the tribe. John thought Charlie greedy and selfish.

John could not become a medicine man until he was thirty without breaking the tradition of his ancestors. He lived by his late father's admonition: "For the young to learn; for the mature to practice." His father had told him that in the young the lust of the body made the profession dangerous, for he might succumb to the seductive outline of a sick girl's breast and betray his trust as a doctor. He might also, in anger, use his medicines to kill, not heal.

Therefore, while waiting to follow in his father's footsteps, John traveled to the Union of South Africa, where he became a waiter, and a very good one, according to Dr. Sachs. Having no money for trains, John had walked the three hundred miles from Manyikaland to the border of the Union of South Africa. It took him two months to do this.

He worked in small hotels, first in the town of Pietersburg, then in Johannesburg. He fled to the latter city when an elderly white spinster lied and accused him of trying to rape her (he had merely bent down to pick up her dressing gown which had dropped off her shoulders as she stood in the hall). Knowing the white police would never take the word of a black, the owner of the hotel advised John to leave the city.

He met Maggie while she was working as a maid in a hotel in Pietersburg. He felt sorry for her because of her crippled leg and, after much persuasion by her, including a visit to her village, where her mother promised Maggie's beautiful younger sister as John's second wife (also a tribal custom), he agreed to marry Maggie. They were never very happy together; Maggie was slovenly and lazy, wanting only to stay in bed day and night, resting her ever-growing bulk.

John had occasional affairs, even living with other women temporarily, until he became a medicine man. Then he remained true to Maggie, for faithfulness was expected of all medicine men. Three things were forbidden to a medicine man, he informed Dr. Sachs: sleeping with any woman but his wife; eating a sheep, because it is not a clever animal; and touching a pig with his hands when it was dead or eating its flesh, because pig meat spoils medicines.

John told Dr. Sachs that his father and mother, who had died during the influenza epidemic of 1918 (which the blacks blamed on the whites), would often come back from the dead to speak with him. In the book, Dr. Sachs explained that for John, as for all Africans, there was no rigid dividing line between the living and the dead, no conception of a hereafter. The dead continued to exist in this world in the form of "midzimu," the spirits of one's ancestors, and thus John believed that his ancestors spoke to him, giving him advice and help. This, said Dr. Sachs, was an interesting form of what psychoanalysts call total introjection of an object. It enabled John to retain within himself his lost father and mother, so dear and vital to him. He saw them as living in their former huts in the village.

Dr. Sachs was struck, he said, by how little John gave himself a chance to think through anything by himself, to reach his own decisions. Always he appealed to his dead mother or father for help, thus remaining emotionally an infant, since they, though dead, remained accessible whenever he needed them, as omniscient as God. (This is the child's view of his parents.)

John belonged to the Anglican Church, having attended the missionary school run by a priest in his native village. There he had learned English.

In recalling some of the experiences in his early life, John told how, on his mother's death, he was so terrified that he screamed and carried on in a wild frenzy. He did not want to live with her gone. He fell sick with a fever, was ill for a year, and everyone thought he would die, but he finally recovered.

He grew up knowing that, according to the tribal taboos, he must never marry or have sexual intercourse with a girl who belonged to the same clan, or had the same "mutupo," which, in his words, was "the animal who protects the man." Every son had his own special "mutupo" which he inherited from his father. John's was "soko," the monkey. To sleep with a girl who had the same "mutupo" was like sleeping with your sister, he explained to Dr. Sachs. When John met a girl, the first thing he asked her was what "mutupo" she was. If she was "soko," he could not make love to her but had to treat her like a brother or father. He had had a woman "properly," as he put it, when he was twelve, but he had never really felt in love with a woman, and certainly not with Maggie, who grew more and more burdensome to him.

Maggie's father, George, was a very cruel man, according to John. He described how he watched George officiate at circumcision rites. John interpreted these rites as cruelties imposed on the young boys by the older people who were jealous and wanted to kill the boys, and that was why they "cut" them.

Dr. Sachs pointed out that, through John's experiences, he discovered an interesting variation of the Oedipus triangle which clarified John's irrational fear of George and, as a rule, of every man in authority, whether white or black. Dr. Sachs explained that normally, in a boy, his love for his mother brings out resentment and hostility against the father, a feeling from which the boy later frees himself by becoming like his father. But John did not have this outlet because his father died when he was six, at a time when Oedipal wishes are strongest.

Also, John, like some African children, was breast-fed until the age of four. During these years he was literally in constant contact with his mother, either at her breast or carried on her back. At night he, not his father, shared the hut with her, because sexual relations between husband and wife were forbidden during the period of breast feeding. Then suddenly, when he was four, his mother's breast was taken away from him and he was sent to another hut. His father appeared out of the blue, so to speak, to usurp his place with his mother.

The Oedipal drama, thus, was more severe for John than for the average white boy, who has a chance to know and love his father, Dr. Sachs explained. The sudden intrusion of a big, godlike stranger into his life at the age of four increased John's resentment over the loss of his mother. Dr. Sachs said that, luckily for John, he found in Charlie, his stepfather, a good substitute for his hostile emotions after his father died.

The long period of breast feeding and the father's absence from the hut had a retarding effect on John's psychological development, as it does on many an African child in his fight for emotional independence, Dr. Sachs said. He added, however, that he thought this important psychological factor counts but little compared to the poverty and starvation, the economic exploitation, and the severe racial discrimination to which black people are subjected to in South Africa.

John's special, personal tragedy, according to Dr. Sachs, was what psychoanalysts call "Hamletism." This psychological phenomenon, he explained, is characterized by indecision and hesitancy in situations that call for direct action. According to certain psychoanalytic interpretations of Shakespeare's play, Hamlet, although realizing he should avenge his father's death, could not bring himself to act quickly because his uncle had done what Hamlet himself unconsciously wished to do (take his father's place). The fact that his mother's new lover was his uncle made Hamlet's internal conflicts overwhelming. He was thrown unaware into the old Oedipus conflict normally resolved at his age. The reality fulfilled Hamlet's forbidden, repressed desires, and this was the cause of his tragic fate.

John's external situation was much like Hamlet's, Dr. Sachs pointed out. John was not a prince, but he was the son of a famous medicine man and had an illustrious ancestry of doctors and chiefs. John's father also died in mysterious circumstances; he had heard hints that his father was poisoned by his uncle for killing his younger brother. Also, like Hamlet, John's uncle married his mother. And, like Hamlet, who loved his mother deeply and, according to Dr. Sachs, had been unable to wean himself from her, John had the same difficulty because of the four year period of breast feeding.

During the analysis there emerged a number of John's superstitions, fears, and beliefs that proved similar to those of most children the world over. For one thing, he believed in the power of magic as he "threw the bones." The "bones" consisted of twenty-eight pieces, including an elephant bone, tortoise bone; bones of a buck, a mamba, a normal sheep, goat, pig, and hyena; bones of a castrated sheep, calf, lion, and baboon; and cattle feet. The interpretation depended upon how the bones fell after he "threw" them—whether the convex surfaces were upward and "closed" or down and "open," and also upon the mutual position of male and female bones of the same species and their relation to the bones of other animals. John also threw six nutshells and six dominoes and used two big horns, which he would rub in his hands for a minute or two.

Like a child, John believed that good or evil could be done to people from a distance—contact was not necessary in order to poison or kill someone; a poisoner could kill from any place. One's wish alone held the power.

Also like a child, John believed in ghosts, in that his ancestors lived on in spirit form, he thought. Again like a child, he projected all his troubles onto other people—it was the fault of his ancestors, or evil spirits, or the white man, or just bad luck.

As happens when people project, scapegoats have to be found before the illness, or bad luck, or curse disappears. For instance, when twins are born in some African tribes, it is considered an omen of catastrophe and produces panic until the twins are killed.

Dr. Sachs was amazed at the similarity between much primitive symbolism and Freudian dream symbols, and also at how universal are the representations in the unconscious mind of sexual activities. After telling one dream, John compared a knife which appeared in the dream to the use of his penis in sex with his wife. This, said Dr. Sachs, showed how, in the unconscious, the male organ could be symbolized by a weapon such as a knife.

The reality of the sex life of the African bore little resemblance to the popular notion of the potent, lustful black, Dr. Sachs discovered. Most of the women he questioned were frigid, and foreplay was almost unknown to the blacks who lived in the cities. Maggie told him she hated sex, that it meant nothing to her. He doubted if she had ever experienced true sexual pleasure; few women she knew had such pleasure, she said. Dr. Sachs later verified this fact in the course of an investigation carried out among John's patients.

John had difficulty at first expressing any anger, but at one point he became furious at Dr. Sachs because he thought the analyst was responsible for his arrest on a trumped-up charge of murdering twins who had been found dead in an alley in the slums near where he lived. After John was freed, for a while he refused to go to Dr. Sachs's office for treatment. When he did appear, he remained silent and would not talk of his anger. Dr. Sachs explained the workings of the aggressive instinct and the unavoidability of hating those we believe to be hostile to us. Hate, like love, cannot be conquered, he told John, but must emerge in one way or another. Gradually he convinced John of this, and, he said, the months of treatment that followed were the most successful of all.

Dr. Sachs drove John and his family back to his village in Rhodesia when John got into trouble in Johannesburg. There, with the people with whom he had grown up, he planned to serve as a medicine man. When he left John, Dr. Sachs did not expect to see him again. But driving back to Johannesburg, about three hundred miles from the village, his car broke down and he had to stay for a week in a small village while spare parts were brought in from Johannesburg.

As he drove away, his car finally fixed, he suddenly saw John walking along the main road outside the village with his son, Daniel. He stopped to ask what had happened. Dr. Sachs realized his departure depressed John more than he thought it would, for John said he had started to drink heavily.

John had demanded that a young girl in his village, with whom he had fallen in love, be brought to his hut. He spent a night of wild passion with her, as is possible, said Dr. Sachs, "only for a love-starved man." John had forgotten to ask her "mutupo" and when he did the next morning, she replied, "soko." John had, in effect, committed the crime of incest. Shocked, he sent the girl away and decided he could no longer remain in the village and would have to return to Johannesburg.

Dr. Sachs commented that flight had always been John's solution to any problem, and once again he was running away from a conflict. He had always depended on extraordinary luck to save him, and when it failed, he would run. Renunciation and flight were his choices in any situation requiring strength of will and endurance of pain.

John also could never say no, even when it was necessary to do so; he preferred to make promises he knew he could not keep. He had not reached that stage of personality development that belongs to the mature man who is not afraid of being assertive or submissive, active or passive, as the occasion demands, at the same time avoiding extremes in any direction.

In addition to his personal problems, John had another tragedy which hovers over almost every African, Dr. Sachs said. His book not only describes John's psychological development, but his feelings about the mistreatment of the natives by the whites who, according to Dr. Sachs, feared and scorned the blacks, jailed them on trumped-up charges, beat them on the slightest pretext, required them to possess innumerable passes to go out at night or from one place to another, and exacted a large tax which most of them could not pay, whereupon they were thrown into jail. Dr. Sachs maintained that the clash of living in two worlds, one white, the other black, caused sharp conflicts for every African, all of whom led double lives in the full sense of the psychological concept. The most remote village had its contacts with European civilization through missionaries, government officials, traders, and labor recruiters. The lure, often the necessity, of earning money, of acquiring possessions like the white man, brought the African to the cities from the most distant corners of the continent. There he met, as a rule, exploitation and brutality, according to Dr. Sachs, and was forced to live in slum areas.

Also, many Africans lived by two conflicting codes of morals and laws and prayed to two gods (in this case to Mwari and Jesus Christ). John put a lot of psychic energy into trying to find a way out of this dilemma. Dr. Sachs said the white man insisted on keeping the Africans enslaved to the traditions of their fathers on the pretext that a gulf of two thousand years separated black from white, thus withholding emancipation from the blacks.

Dr. Sachs accompanied John to some of the meetings where educated black men spoke to the young men and women of Africa, protesting the injustices done by the white world. He mentioned one speaker, a tall, dignified black man, who made a deep impression on everyone when he said there must be no desire for revenge on the part of the black man, who, no less than the white, had to be a partner in the destiny of Africa. "Leave fighting to animals," he said. "Suffer quietly. But learn." He urged the Africans to become educated and civilized so that the white man would look at them differently.

Dr. Sachs helped John all he could on his return to Johannesburg, where John continued to practice as a medicine man. He noticed a growing assertiveness and rebellion in John, the formerly quiet, compassionate doctor. For a while it looked as though John had rebelled too strongly, for Maggie appealed to Dr. Sachs for help when John started to give people herbs for evil purposes, to wish someone dead, and became part of a gang of young delinquents who stole. At one point, John even wished to poison Maggie. He stole medicine from Dr. Sachs's office labeled "poison" and put it in her tea, believing it would kill her. When he confessed this to Dr. Sachs, the analyst assured him that it had only been sleeping medicine.

But after this revelation from John that he could be a murderer, Dr. Sachs felt stunned. He never once suspected John capable of such a crime. On the other hand, he admitted he was pleased to find that the old John, lacking courage and endurance, was giving way to a new man who was not afraid of asserting himself and the instinct to fight his way through life. Dr. Sachs continued to see John and Maggie, who also came for help, until John was able to turn his rebellion into more constructive channels.

When John's treatment ended, Dr. Sachs felt a change had taken place in him. His friends also felt it, and Maggie was definite about it. She said he had stopped drinking and sleeping around with other women, and brought money home. He built a chicken yard in their small home and even planted a vegetable patch.

In addition to being a medicine man, John now became an effective propagandist. He addressed small groups (assemblies of more than ten Africans were then forbidden by the authorities throughout South Africa) and pointed out the dangers of violence, which would lose for them the sympathy of those whites who stood behind the Africans. John also worked hard to get better living conditions for his people.

Dr. Sachs described John as feeling that the future held promise of better things to come. When Dr. Sachs, in August 1945, said good-bye to John before leaving for a visit to America, John did not seem despondent at his departure as he had been when, once before, Dr. Sachs left Africa for a while. John asked Dr. Sachs to tell the people in the United States, particularly the Negroes, how alone and isolated the natives of Africa felt in their misery, with no one in the world to whom to appeal.

John was looking to a new vision, a bond with his people in America, said Dr. Sachs, and he realized how important to John this hope was. He promised he would do what he could to help him realize it. Thus it was, said Dr. Sachs, that the story of John, a psychoanalytic study which he originally planned to write only for a limited number of scientists, became the story of John the man, to be read by everyone.

# Index

Using twelve original case histories by pioneers in psychoanalytic theory, Miss Freeman traces the development of this peculiarly modern science from its beginnings in the last century—as Freud's private province—up to the present day. She has selected each study carefully, for its particular contribution to psychoanalytic knowledge, and introduces each with lucid explanatory comment.

Although several of Freud's long studies are well known, the works of some of the other figures are relatively unknown to the public. They have added immeasurably to the art and science of psychoanalysis but have remained tucked away in medical books and journals. Represented in the collection are the contributions of such men as Stewart, Lorand, Eidelberg, Knight, and Grotjahn—to name only a few.

Not all of the cases assembled here are typical of classic psychoanalytic procedure, for a few represent psychotherapy in practice, but all are based on psychoanalytic principles, and all illustrate psychic processes in simple language. Such terms as repression, regression, transference, projection, sublimation take on new meaning for the reader when they are exemplified in real situations.